The Colour of Life

Jill Williams and Barbara Long

©Jill Williams and Barbara Long 2008

All rights reserved

No part of this publication may be reproduced,
stored in a retrieval system, or transmitted
in any form or by any means, without the prior
permission in writing of the publisher,
nor be otherwise circulated in any form of binding
or cover other than that in which it is published
and without a similar condition including this condition
being imposed on the subsequent purchaser.

First published in Great Britain in 2008
Pen Press
25, Eastern Place
Brighton, BN2 1GJ

ISBN 13: 978-1-906710-01-9

Printed and bound in the UK
A catalogue record of this book is available from
the British Library

Cover design by Jacqueline Abromeit

In Loving Memory

MARK

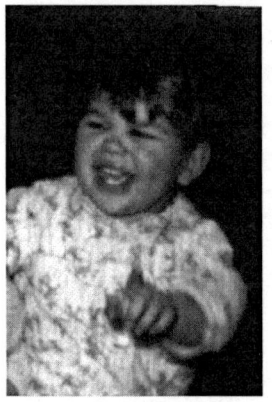

April 1, 1963 to March 2 1986

Foreword

We are white Europeans who are proud to have discovered our black African ancestors.

"After the birth of my son in 1963, the hospital nurse began questioning me about my husband's nationality. I realised then that our son's skin was darker than ours." Jill Williams.

Years later my Aunt and I began a journey of discovery. We were told stories by elderly relatives that our ancestors were African slaves. Intrigued by this information we set out to see if the stories were in fact true.

This book, *The Colour of Life* is the result of a twenty three year research journey into the lives of our ancestors, a journey which took us to the Tuaregs of Niger, the slave trade in Sierra Leone, the workhouses and Rampton Hospital in Britain. Most of the names are factual. Some events are fictional to give continuity.

Chapter 1

Shakina was born in Niger of Tuareg parents, descendants of the diverse groups of people who originated in North Africa. Handsome, friendly and impressively self-sufficient people famed as camel riders, groups of these people moved from the north hoping for a more prosperous land in the south.

The Turareg men wear long robes called a Boubous and because of the indigo dyes used in the material they are known as the Blue Men. A large turban that covers the entire head except the eyes is never removed, even in front of family members. Males are not considered men until they have made the journey across the Sahara with the camel caravan and returned home safely.

Taureg tradition is that an amulet made of brass and copper can heal injuries and prevent new ones from occurring, and are also given as a gift to a Taureg bride on her wedding day to bring harmony to her and her husband.

Young children in various ethnic groups receive distinctive facial scars in elaborate ceremonies which often last for days, after which the wounds are rubbed with ash to make them darker.

A celebration called the Cure Salee was a homecoming for their migrations far to the south during the dry season.

After gathering at a place near In-Gall the Tauregs would rest, fatten their animals and enjoy each others company through camel racing, music and dancing. The men standing in a circle, chanting and swaying to the music, would try to impress the on-looking young women who were hoping to be chosen, sometimes for a night, sometimes for life. These were the customs of Shanika's homeland, her culture, her life.

How different it was to become.

When she was old enough to understand, her parents had warned her of the dangers of being captured. "There are those who prey on our people, abducting them, and selling them into slavery", her father explained.

"And," he continued, "it's not only the Europeans, Africans also capture Africans of other tribes and sell them to the Europeans. Our own people, the Tuaregs are known for doing just that."

Shakina sat at her father's feet, listening intently.

Her father spoke softly, a sad lilt to his voice, "Many years ago slave traders set up bases along the West African coast. There they purchased slaves from Africans and paid for them with firearms and other goods. Some of the northern nations—England, France, Denmark, Holland and Portugal— established slave trading posts on our Western coast. Many of our own people as well as those of other tribes have become involuntary immigrants to other lands."

"Some resisted, fleeing the slave forts but of course, they were soon recaptured." He sighed, shrugged, and continued. "Others mutinied aboard slave trading vessels, or threw themselves into the sea. Many ran away from their owners and formed maroon societies, or sought and succeeded in gaining freedom through legal means such as 'good service,' self-purchase or military service. Sadly most learned to survive in servitude."

It was the slavers who altered the course of Shakina's life and those of the villagers' with whom in she lived. One day in 1790 the air suddenly filled with the sound of men shouting for their wives, women crying for their men, and the frightened screams of children. The slave traders had come. Children tried running and hiding but they were soon captured.

Terrified people were dragged from their homes, bound, chained and driven off like cattle to market. For weeks the slavers pushed and prodded their victims along until they reached the coast of Sierra Leone. There they forced the captured Africans into warehouse-like prisons until slave ships arrived at the port. Once the slave ships were moored, the slavers loaded their human cargo into small boats, snapping whips at their backs as they forced them to row to the moorings. These were the first steps in the long journey from Africa to America. So went Shakina and her parents; she was fifteen years old.

Each morning as the sun began to rise the slaves were brought up from below decks, shackled together with iron chains and given their first meal of the day which consisted of the cheapest foodstuffs available, usually large beans used to feed horses. These were boiled until they became soft and dished up to the slaves with occasional pieces of raw meat thrown in to keep them "healthy". Fifteen minutes later the slaves were cramped together in the belly of the ship.

During storms, of which there were many during the long sea passage, the captives remained below deck day and night in holds that were filthy and dark, breathing air that was filled with the overpowering stench of death. Human beings stuffed between decks in spaces less than two feet high where they were forced to lie on their backs, their heads between the legs of others. Unable to move, this resulted in them lying in each other's faeces, vomit, urine and blood. The heat became unbearable, and disease spread quickly. Smallpox and yellow fever raged through the ship. Often the living remained chained to the bodies of the dead until the corpses were thrown overboard.

Preferring death to the ship's hell many slaves jumped overboard knowing they would drown, so desperate were they to escape this life. Others tried to starve themselves to death but their captors thwarted them by using a device to open their mouths which contained live coals. Iron muzzles and whippings were everyday cruelties. Women and adolescent girls were often used for "bed-warming". A crew member would unshackle a woman during the night and take her to the crew's quarters where they would beat her, forcing her to have sex with one or more of them.

As water ran low and disease raged, the captain decided to throw terminally ill slaves overboard. Insurance would not cover sick slaves or those who had died of disease but it would pay for slaves lost through drowning, so the captain ordered many chained Africans to be thrown overboard. By the time the slave ship had reached its destination, the captain and crew had murdered many people in this way.

The ocean crossing took fifty-one days; over seven weeks of high winds and rough seas breaking over the bow, Shakina and many others were seasick for at least half of the journey. Day and night she heard the anguished cries of her people. One morning two of the ship's crew came and took the chains from her father and by lifting her head and turning as far as her own chains would allow Shakina could see that her father had died. Her mother cried and wailed for her husband. Her reward was a whip flaying her bare back.

Every slave soon learned that a visiting crewman meant either someone had died or that it was time for the living to "entertain" the crew. Slavers took their captives on deck at three each afternoon to perform an exercise the traders called "dancing the slaves" where the slaves were forced to jump up and down still shackled together. Those who lacked enthusiasm were whipped and by the time the "dancing" had finished many black backs oozed blood while the raw flesh on their ankles bled from the leg irons. Men, women and children had to dance to a rhythm that was played on tin pans or kettles, after which the slaves would be taken back below decks to lie in their own filth. This ship was Shakina's living hell for nearly two months with the air un-breathable and the heat unbearable.

When the ship reached port Shakina was pushed into a stall which was similar to a cattle pen along with her mother, two other women, five men and six children. The slavers had rubbed oil into their bodies to make their skin shiny. They then applied hot tar to the scars caused by the daily whippings making the slaves look healthy, in order to fetch the best price.

To stop the rich white bidders seeing the "stock" too soon, slavers covered the front of the stall with cloth. As the overseer pulled back the curtain for the first sale of the day, bidders surged forward.

"Show them how you trot," the overseer demanded. "Show them how you jump! C'mon you bucks… Show it, wench!"

Buyers pawed them as if they were less than human, whilst the overseer gave a running narration on the attributes of each slave:

"This here wench is half-blind, but her back's strong enough… This boy's been employed as a porter, gentlemen…

"This here's Robuck, and he's as attentive and diligent as they come. Not a bad sort...

"Here we have Joey, who's quite a good boy. He'll make a trustworthy servant...

"Missy's a quiet woman, a little discontented but a tolerable servant…

"Eliza's a well-behaved young girl and already a good washer."

One woman begged to be allowed to go to the stall where her young children were being held. "Oh please master," she wailed, "they are my children. Please let me go with them." Her cries went unheeded. Her children were sold.

A slave's value was set according to size, age, sex and strength with the slaves who looked the strongest fetching the highest prices, followed by child slaves. Bidders rubbed their fingers over the teeth of any slave they were interested in. They prodded, pushed and poked them. They then started haggling with the traders to get the cheapest prices, and the most able-bodied slaves. The fate of hundreds of frightened men, women and children was decided in a language they barely understood. For many the only hope of release was the grave.

Most "owners" gave their slaves minimal clothing: children a shirt, the men a pair of trousers, and a dress for the women. Slaves finding themselves in the hands of more kindly masters would be allowed a jacket or overcoat, a wool hat once in two or three years and a pair of coarse shoes. Slaves were housed in huts, out-houses or barns built of rough boards with small openings in the side for windows and an earth floor. Men would get one shack, the women another. The beds were mostly a collection of straw or rags. Sometimes, the better-off slaves would be given a single blanket for a cover. Eight to ten people huddled together in a single shack.

Owners had their own different ways of administering punishment. Recaptured escapees often had cowbells attached to them. This would consist of a band of iron fastened around the neck, with a hinge behind and a padlock hanging under the slave's chin so that with every movement the cowbells rang. Others were whipped, after which salt would be rubbed into their open wounds.

One slave who worked in the kitchens of a "big house" was caught eating one of the biscuits she had baked. Her punishment was to have a needle pushed through her bottom lip, upon which the hem of her skirt was then hung. Unable to stand upright because of the weight of the skirt on the needle, she spent three weeks stooped over, constantly dribbling as she couldn't swallow her saliva.

Chapter 2

Shakina and her mother were sold to a wealthy British couple, Mr and Mrs Augustine Robertson-Smyth, who owned homes in America and Britain. Slaveholders grew rich through the cotton industry and the Robertson-Smyths' prosperity was a result of this trade. Augustine's grandfather purchased his first plantation in 1700. Slaves worked the fields and lived their lives under constant supervision from the overseers and were not allowed to congregate or learn to read or write.

Both women lost their true Niger identities when two days after being sold Shakina became "Charlotte" and her mother was re-named "Eliza."

The Robertson-Smyths had their rules. Charlotte broke the most important one the day she arrived at the house. The rule was "speak only when spoken to". Over-awed at the size of the family's colonial style house and grounds, Charlotte exclaimed to her mother, "I have never seen anything as beautiful as this house Mama." She received two lashes, learning quickly never to repeat the "offence".

Mother and daughter worked from 5.00 am until 7.45 in the evening. Eliza worked in the kitchen cooking for the Robertson-Smyths and their four children. Her other duties included cleaning silver, washing and ironing as and when she was told to. Charlotte was to be an upstairs maid, responsible for the mistress's clothes and every other need. She laboured under the watchful eye of another slave called Millie. Millie had been sold four times, and no longer knew where her family was. The task of supervising Charlotte overjoyed her, and as time went by she came to think of her as the daughter she'd never had.

Huge beds and pillows filled the main bedroom. The adornments included fancy spreads, pillows finished with lace and embroidery and soft fancy cushions while long heavy drapes hung at every window. Fine brushes, mirrors and make-up were arranged on an ornate dressing table. Charlotte stood in awe when she saw all the finery.

"Now watch me careful gal", Millie said, as she put Mrs Robertson-Smyth's clothes in the cupboard adjoining the main bedroom, "Watch and learn. This is how the Mistress likes her clothes to be put away." Charlotte gazed at the many clothes and shoes that the cupboard held. She wished that she had clothes like that.

Millie taught her well. Within weeks Charlotte knew the order in which to hang the beautiful silk dresses, how to fold undergarments properly and lay them neatly in the huge chest of drawers.

Under the older woman's instructions Charlotte quickly learnt the routine, a routine which took place every day, starting with emptying the chamber pot, washbasins and jugs after the Robertson-Smyths left their bedroom in the mornings. Millie showed her how to make the bed, squaring off the corners of the blankets, plumping up the pillows and making sure that the openings of the pillow cases faced the bed's centre. She demonstrated how to put the counterpane on, making sure to tuck any surplus neatly under the pillows.

"In the early evening, about 7pm," said Millie, "take the counterpane off, turn the blankets down and place their night attire on the bed."

Charlotte's mother resented the harshness of the new world she had been forced into and would often rebel. They whipped her almost daily. Her daughter watched and wished her mother could live with the Robertson-Smyths' rules but at the same time she felt proud of her; she admired the way she stood upright and dry-eyed while being chastised. Even when the whip snaked across her bare back before curling round and cutting into her ribs, Eliza refused to weep.

Come evening when work was over, Charlotte, along with her mother and Millie would walk past the barn where the male slaves were housed at night. The female accommodation was a smaller barn that was located further down the track at the back of the house. Every night they would listen to the heavy lock on the barn door snapping shut as they were locked in. The only light was from the moon seeping through the cracks of the barn, stretching its silver-coloured rays across the floor. By this light Millie and Charlotte dabbed the festering wounds on Eliza's back, using the hem of her dress and a little of the rationed water. Once her mother was comfortable Charlotte would sit cross-legged on her straw bed and watch as hundreds of tiny insects floated through the shafts of moonlight. The two older women would whisper their dreams to each other, dreams of escape back to their beloved Africa.

Deep down in their hearts they knew that was all it was: a dream. For them there was no escape.

Life changed very little over the next few years. Charlotte grew into a strikingly good-looking woman. She was long-limbed with thick black hair that when not pulled back under her white mop cap, framed her face in a halo of tiny curls. She had learnt many English words, mainly from the youngest child of the house. Lydia Robertson-Smyth always made a point of speaking to Charlotte whenever she saw her.

At first Charlotte would just nod her head, unsure of what she should do. Lydia soon realised this and would smile at

Charlotte and ask: "What is your country like? What traditions do you follow?" Or "Describe your houses and the clothes that you wore."

Lydia had never heard of the Berber language called Tamashegh which was the language spoken by the Tuaregs. Speaking broken English and drawing rough pictures in the dirt at the back of the house, Charlotte told the girl about her homeland.

"Everything", she said "is dictated by the needs of our cattle. Ensuring that they grow big and fat and then trading them is all we have. We eat rice or wheat, sometimes we also have meat. Girls get married after the age of fourteen, some as late as twenty-one. After this age it is very difficult to be chosen as a wife."

At this point Charlotte looked off into the distance. "I was to marry a handsome young man but …." Her voice trailed off.

Lydia touched her hand, and brought her back to the present... Charlotte smiled. "The older women teach children proverbs and our alphabet, the *tifinagh* and we are all encouraged to play a one-stringed violin, called an *imzad*."

"I thought it was all sand and sun," said Lydia.

"Well, there are miles and miles of sand and endless days of sun," Charlotte said, "the Tenere is a vast arid desert with sand dunes running continuously for miles, rising in places to be taller than the tallest man. Very little grows there."

At that moment they heard a man's voice in the distance: "Lydia where are you?"

"Tell me the rest later," Lydia said smiling at Charlotte, before running down to the stables to join her father.

At last the young slave had a "friend". But Lydia was a friend only at a distance. Charlotte knew her place.

Ten years later, having made their fortune in America, the Robertson-Smyths returned to London. Many wealthy plantation owners went back to London, taking their fortunes and their personal slaves. Young, exotic black servants dressed in fancy costumes with metal collars around their necks were like fashion accessories for London's elite.

The Robertson-Smyths spared their servants the indignities of neck collars and fancy costumes, but only because they were costly. They had already paid for two sets of indoor clothes plus a set of outdoor clothes and decided that for lowly servants that was enough. Among the slaves accompanying the family were Charlotte, her mother and a newly bought twenty-year-old groom named Ben.

Chapter 3

At the beginning of the nineteenth century London was the largest city in the world. Chinese, Irish, Indian, African and Italian immigrants were all carving out their own communities.

Charlotte arived in Mayfair, London in October 1800 when the weather was damp, misty and grey. In the distance she could see trees with foliage turning deep hues of orange, red and yellow. She looked at the house in amazement. It was so tall she had to bend her head back to see the roof. All the houses on the road had red tile roofs, large sash windows, decorated entrance ways and were fronted by wrought-iron railings.

A heavily built man of about fifty, with small narrow eyes and a ruddy complexion opened the heavy main door. As the Robertson-Smyths stepped past him, Tom bowed his head slightly. The Master nodded at the newcomers, and said: "There they are Tom, take them round to the back entrance and then tell Anna to show them to their rooms."

Anna escorted the slaves though a small scullery that led into the kitchen. Fixed to one wall of the kitchen was a large wooden block on which hung a variety of bells. These would ring when something was required upstairs. In the centre of the kitchen stood a huge wooden table flanked by eight chairs.

A large stove with ovens to the side took up almost the whole of the smaller wall. Brass kettles and pots hung from pothooks. The larger wall was home to an enormous dresser that held a variety of dinner and tea services, and gleaming as if they were new were matching serving dishes, meat plates and soup bowls.

Ben, Charlotte and Eliza were led through a door which was situated at the back of the kitchen, down a long passage to a narrow flight of stairs. These were the "back stairs" for use by the servants. Climbing the stairs they found themselves on a small landing.

"The room to the right is Tom's and mine and you're over there boy," Anna said pointing to Ben. "You will be in the room straight ahead there," she said to the two women. "Right, now you've got ten minutes to catch your breath, get yourselves presentable then it's time to get to work. Come on, get a move on."

Charlotte and Eliza looked around their room which contained two small beds with horsehair mattresses between which stood a chest of drawers. On the chest was a washbasin and jug, both cracked. A cupboard with one door slightly higher than the other was leaning against the wall opposite the tiny window. A chamber pot stood on the floor. The room was quite tiny, but a bedroom nonetheless, which was more than they'd had in America. Quickly they put their meagre belongings away and made their way down to the scullery.

Ladies in fine clothes and expensive shoes called on the Robertson-Smyths most days of the week and life in the Mayfair house became a hive of activity. The servants would serve tea and cakes on silver trays with matching teapot, sugar bowl, spoons and cream jug. Charlotte smiled with pride whenever someone commented about the shine on the silver. Day by day, life became a little better for Charlotte and Eliza; there were fewer beatings and their masters addressed them in a more civil manner.

Tom had become very friendly towards Charlotte. Often when out of sight of the Master and his wife, he would circle her waist with his arm or squeeze her buttocks. His loins tingled whenever he saw her and he was determined to have her before long. With her pert breasts, slim waist and full thick lips she would be a welcome change from Anna.

"Anna never looked as good as that," he mused ,"not even in her younger days."

Whenever he saw Charlotte and the young groom Ben, shyly glancing at each other he could feel himself becoming red with anger. He'd noticed them sitting close at the big kitchen table, their hands touching as they passed the serving dishes to each other.

"I'll taste her sweetness first," Tom vowed to himself with a grin.

Time passed and soon it was mid December 1800 which meant several parties were held at the Robertson-Smyths' house celebrating the Christmas period. The drawing room was decked with shiny streamers, big bows in red and gold and tiny candles. Standing on the long cupboard by the door were bottles of rum, beer and cider to wash down the hams and cheeses that would be brought up from the kitchen.

The preparations kept Charlotte and her mother busy from morning till night. There was washing, ironing, silver to polish and the guest bedrooms to prepare. One morning after cleaning the parlour, Charlotte heard her mother calling, "Please help me someone, I don't feel at all well."

Charlotte ran down the stairs passing Anna on the way.

"Don't you dare run in this house," she bellowed. Charlotte ignored her. Anna's instinct knew there was something terribly wrong. Eliza had gone an awful grey colour and was lying on the floor was gasping for breath.

There was nothing anyone could do. Death often came quickly in those days and it had now taken Eliza. She was buried in a pauper's grave at the back of a church about a mile from the Robertson-Smyths' home. The servants didn't attend the burial but gave Charlotte a holly sprig, which she placed on the grave along with her own wreath. She had spent a whole evening lovingly shaping and bending holly, which she had picked from the tree at the back of the garden. When she had finished, her fingers were cut and bleeding but she didn't feel the pain. Losing her beloved mother had left her numb.

Chapter 4

It was January 1801 and the thaw had started at last. The icicles that had formed on the windows were slowing melting and life in the Mayfair household continued much the same as it always had done.

Charlotte was now about 24 years old, the Robertson-Smyths had decided that her Birthday was 3rd January, that being the day they had bought her. She had grown into a beautiful woman, graceful and upright with a slight touch of aloofness. Male guests to the house often commented amongst themselves as to "what a beauty for a black woman" she was. They were not the only ones who noticed her. Tom's interest had never faded and he watched her whenever he could. Watched her as she took the laundry upstairs, her hips swaying with every step she took. He noticed her breasts pushing against the material of her apron, as if they were trying to show themselves. He couldn't get Charlotte out of his mind.

The servants were below stairs one afternoon sitting round the big table that dominated the kitchen when Charlotte accidentally spilt tea whilst pouring it into Tom's cup. Tom raised his eyebrows and started sighing. Charlotte shot him a look of contempt. Too late, she realised her error.

Pushing his chair back from the table with such force that it fell backwards, Tom pulled Charlotte by the arm and dragged her to the scullery whilst informing the others at the table that she was going to be punished for being so clumsy.

Ben protested, "It was just an accident and you shouldn't be punishing her, that's for the Master to deal with."

"Mind your mouth and your business Ben", spat Anna.

She thought Ben paid Charlotte far too much attention and it was time the girl was bought down a peg or two. The house rules of the Robertson-Smyths were that single servants of the opposite sex were not to get familiar with each other. It interfered with work duties.

Closing the scullery door behind them Tom took a leather strap from the cupboard and holding Charlottes hair with one hand, he pulled her head down and beat her across her buttocks. Although her frock stopped some of the pain she could still feel the sting of each lash, biting her lip so as not to cry, Charlotte began punching and kicking trying to break free. Tom was enjoying this and pulled her hair harder, he liked to see her writhing, thought it a pity she wasn't naked. Pulling her head up while still holding on to her hair he dropped the strap and grabbed one of Charlotte's breasts, kneading it roughly. She opened her mouth to shout but at that moment he pushed his tongue into her mouth. His hand left her breast and made its way down her back to her bruised buttock. He pulled her to him, rubbing himself against her leg.

Suddenly Anna was knocking furiously on the scullery door,

"It's time for Charlotte to turn down the Robertson-Smyths bed covers. Send her upstairs."

Quickly, Tom stepped away. Charlotte straightened her mop cap, smoothed her clothes down and went to finish her daily duties.

"I'll be with you in a moment", Tom called out to his wife while at the same time adjusting his trousers in the hope that no one would notice his erection. This done he walked out of the scullery and over to the kitchen table where he sat down and finished drinking his tea.

Charlotte pondered over what she should do about Tom and that evening she explained to Anna what had happened, adding, "He is your husband; could you tell him not to touch me like that again? He has no right to do such things to me."

Anna's face turned red with fury, but she said nothing.

Before the servants sat down to breakfast the following morning, Anna shouted at Charlotte "Go to the scullery now!" "Tom", she continued, "I'd like you there as well". Once inside the scullery, away from prying ears, Anna relayed everything Charlotte had told her.

"I have no idea what she's talking about," replied Tom, "I never laid a finger on her".

"You lying black hussy," Anna screeched as she swiped her hand across Charlotte's face before picking up her skirts and flouncing back into the kitchen.

Behind the scullery door, Tom grinned at Charlotte and tweaked one of her breasts before joining his wife in the kitchen. Tom was planning his next move, having already decided that Charlotte would love what he was going to do to her next. It was just a matter of when and where. Just the thought of her made him tingle with excitement.

Two weeks later Anna caught flu. Tom seized his chance. It was 1.35am and with his wife in a deep sleep that accompanies flu he quietly closed their bedroom door behind him.

Charlotte woke with a start but before she had chance to call out, Tom's hand was over her mouth.

"Anna didn't believe you last time," he said in a hushed whisper, "and she wont this time either. In fact, no one will ever believe anything that you, a black servant girl, says."

He slid his trousers down and tugged at Charlotte's night wear, tearing the tapes from the front. She heard him groan as he put his lips over one nipple. Tom smiled to himself; he could be with her most of the night, Anna wouldn't wake till the morning. His hands travelled down to Charlottes inner thighs, felt the mound he had so often dreamt about, he could hardly control him-self now. His fingers probed and pushed. Then he was on top of her, his knees forcing her legs apart, thrusting until he was inside her. The pain was awful and Charlotte thought she was going to be sick.

When she thought nothing could be worse than what she was going through, Tom suddenly flipped her over onto her stomach and an even more painful nightmare began. After what to Charlotte seemed an eternity it was over, Tom stopped and collapsed exhausted on top of her. Sweat dripping from his forehead, his breathing heavy. Tears were streaming down Charlottes cheeks, her body broken and bruised. Before leaving Tom grabbed her ear and while twisting it said with a sneer,

"Don't forget, I will come to you again, whenever I want to".

The first rays of daylight filtered through the small window of her bedroom and Charlotte was still awake. She sat on the bed, her head in her hands, arms and legs bruised, eyes swollen from crying and decided that she should tell her Mistress what had taken place the night before.

Trying to avoid Tom all morning, Charlotte carried on with her work as best she could. Every part of her body ached and despite cleaning herself after the rape and again before she started her daily duties she still felt so dirty. At 10.30am carrying the mid morning tea tray, Charlotte knocked gently on the parlour door. Having been told to enter, she crossed the room and placed the tray on the low table under the window. Turning she asked "Ma'am may I speak to you about a personal matter before pouring the tea?"

A curt nod told her she could do so. Nervously the young girl began telling her what had taken place the night before. When she had finished Mrs Robertson-Smyth sat shaking her head for a few seconds before looking down her nose at Charlotte.

"I have never," she shrieked, "heard such nonsense. Tom has been in my employment long before we went to America. He came with excellent recommendations from the clergy of his local Church. He certainly wouldn't want a nigger like you when he has a loyal hard working wife like Anna."

"Now girl, get back to work, stop lying and don't you ever bother me with such trivial matters again. If you do I will have Mr. Robertson-Smyth remove you from this house. Do you understand me?"

With a flick of a well manicured hand Charlotte was dismissed.

The day seemed to pass so slowly, Charlotte couldn't eat. She still felt sick and every step was agony. Twice Ben had asked her whether she was ill. She desperately wanted to tell him about Tom and what had happened but there was no point, Mrs Robertson-Smyth and Anna had both called her a liar, others probably would too. Tom had not spoken one word to her, but as the working day drew to a close and the last candle in the kitchen had been extinguished, he grinned and told her he would see her later.

Slowly Charlotte trudged upstairs. Once inside her bedroom she put her candle on the windowsill and crawled under the bedcover fully clothed. She was too frightened to get into her bed-gown, too afraid to sleep. Just after midnight she heard the latch on her door being lifted. She kept very still as the door opened about an inch. Then it stopped. Charlotte had pushed the chest of drawers in front of it. Tom put his mouth to the gap between the door and the frame and said in a hoarse whisper, "Tomorrow I will tell Mr. Robertson-Smyth I need the chest.

You know he will give it to me. Then what are you going to do? Anyway I don't mind waiting. What I am going to do to you ,my little black whore, will be worth the wait."

Tom had his plans, but Charlotte also had hers. If she could get down to the scullery where the key to the back entrance was hanging on a hook she could unlock the door and leave. Life in this house would become unbearable now. Tom would make sure of that.

Taking the cover from the bolster, Charlotte gathered the few clothes she owned and placed them inside. Having put on her threadbare cape and her only pair of outdoor shoes, she sat on the bed and waited. Time passed and the house quietened.

Downstairs the kitchen seemed very eerie - the small amount of light from the window was throwing shadows on the walls. Charlotte moved stealthily towards the pantry, took some oatcakes, cheese and a chunk of bread and placed them in the bolster cover. She went through the kitchen into the scullery tiptoeing so as not to make a noise on the stone floor. Taking the key, she unlocked the back door and stepped into the night. She had no idea where she would go.

Her hard work over the years had amounted to nothing but a half sovereign, a few copper coins and a small bundle of clothes.

An hour later the bitter wind had gone though to her bones, Charlotte's teeth were chattering and her nose felt numb. Her hands were so cold she could hardly feel them. Having had no proper sleep for two nights, she felt too weary to walk any further. She could see bare trees and several bushes in the distance and decided that she would go and sit there awhile. Placing her bundle of clothes on the ground between two of the bushes, she lay down next to it. Somewhere nearby a dog was howling and every so often there was a rustle in the undergrowth; hungry rodents looking for food.

Using the bundle of clothes as a makeshift bolster, a very frightened Charlotte drifted into a restless sleep.

The voices of people going about their daily business woke her a few hours later. Some of them walked past her, others glanced at her then quickly looked away. She tided her hair a best she could, but with only the small looking glass that she had taken from the bedroom at Mr & Mrs Robertson-Smyths it was difficult to see whether it looked presentable. Ensuring there was no-one nearby, Charlotte went behind one of the bushes and finished her toiletries. This done, she ran her hands over her clothes hoping that as the day went on the creases in her skirts would fall out. For a brief moment she wondered whether she should go back to the house. She knew she wasn't going to like living like this. At once, images of Tom and what he had done floated around in her head.

No, she wasn't going back.

Chapter 5

Charlotte tried hard to find decent employment, as did so many other people who trod the lonely streets of London, but six weeks after leaving the Robertson-Smyths she was still sleeping under bushes.

She had not left the "posh" area of London, hoping that one of the rich people living there would offer her a position. Twice since leaving the Robertson-Smyths she thought she was going to be offered a position. All would go well until she was asked what position she had held before and why she had left. No one believed her story. With a look of disdain they just closed the door in her face or if she was lucky she would be offered a small coin to scrub the steps of a big house.

Her fingernails were long and filthy. Dirt was ingrained into her hands and face. Clothes that had once been neat and tidy hung in rags and matted hair formed tight clumps against her head. When the rain fell Charlotte would try and find a puddle big enough to rinse the hem of her skirt and wash her hands and face. Sometimes she would find a pond and hitching her skirts she would kneel down and plunge her head into the weed filled water. She rarely wore her cape during the daytime, preferring instead to cover herself with it at nightfall when the air became cooler. Her only shoes had long worn out and she had resorted to hunting through the rubbish thrown out by the rich of the big houses. She had been lucky enough to find a pair, they were far too big for her but at least they had soles on. On some occasions she found scraps of food that had been thrown out, but usually the rats had eaten first.

After knocking on nearly every door Charlotte realised that she wasn't going to find employment in that area. Having no idea where she was or where she was going her days were spent just aimlessly wandering. Her wandering bought her into contact with other vagrants, which is what she had become. At last she didn't feel so lonely and afraid. They would walk the roads by day, deep in thoughts of happier times. Sometimes they would walk in groups of two's and three's, making plans about what they would buy with their wages when they finally found a position.

Most of her new found friends had been vagrants far longer than Charlotte. They warned her of the harsh treatment that would be metered out by the authorities to any one that was homeless and found begging. So they were all very careful and would wait until the early hours of the morning to scavenge. It was the only way they could get food and clothes.

Three and a half years later Charlotte was still living on the streets of London. This once beautiful woman who had endured the cruelty of slavery, the loss of her parents and the degradation of being sexually abused had been forced to beg. She detested doing this and was ever fearful of being caught but she had no option. She knew that the upper class looked down on "her sort", their opinion being that the lack of morality among the poor had bred a culture of poverty.

At times she had managed to find employment but only for an hour or two. In the spring and summer when the rich congregated in London there was a demand for workers but this demand dwindled in the winter. Sweeping dirt or dragging rubbish from the front of someone's house was the only work she was given. She would cringe with embarrassment when with a sneer her "wage" was thrown in the street. If only she could walk away and leave the money where it fell but she knew she couldn't afford to, so on her hands and knees she would crawl until she found it.

On occasions when she had money, she would find a room, sharing it with as many as eight other people, in houses known as "rookeries". These were areas of overcrowded housing tucked from view behind the main richer streets.

The smell in and around these areas was awful. A nauseating mix of sweating horses, dung, and houses crowded with unwashed bodies burning anything they could for cooking, making the air heavy and foul-smelling.

The cobbled streets were full of horse drawn carriages and wagons, the iron shod wooden wheels rattling over the cobbles making a tremendous din. Horse dung littered the streets and dirty-faced urchins with runny noses and no shoes shovelled it into sacks to sell as manure. Many were run over by the wagons, some receiving dreadful injuries.

There were flies everywhere, horse flies that bit everyone and huge bluebottles that invaded everywhere contaminating everything they landed on. The elite required porters, servants, washerwomen and cooks, and the poor who filled those positions needed to live near their employers due to the long hours they were required to work and as a result of this the "rookeries" had grown.

September came and now the days were not so warm nor the sun so strong. Charlotte knew that the well off-folk of London would soon be leaving, going to warmer climates until winter was over and any hope of finding work in the big houses would soon be over. Having been frugal in her spending she had managed to purchase a bar of soap and a comb. Hunting in rubbish she had been asked to move from one of the big houses, had rewarded her with a near decent frock, the hem was frayed and there was a small rip down the front but it fitted her perfectly, showing off her tiny waist and slim hips. She had also found a pair of boots, with tiny buttons on the side. The heels were somewhat worn but to Charlotte, they still looked classy. Sadly there was nothing she could do about her cape, it was threadbare and stained.

The West India Docks had opened in 1802 and as the Docks began to grow, so too did other industries such as engineering and warehousing. With these came the smaller industries such as eating establishments and clothes manufacturers. As with all Docks the area attracted a large calling of ladies whose job was the "oldest profession in the world" large and small, young and old most hating what they had to do for a living.

It was in the area of the Docks that Charlotte found herself one October day. She had washed as thoroughly as she could, considering the conditions she was living in and after combing her hair she had put on her "new" frock and shoes. Her bonnet had seen better days, but she had cleaned it best she could and thought it didn't look too bad. With her head held high she walked through the doors of one of the eating-houses.

There was no name over the door, just the word "FOOD". It wasn't one of the expensive eating places, but was certainly one of the busiest. The first thing Charlotte noticed was the smell of stale tobacco. The interior was small, dingy and dark, the only light coming in through a tiny window which was as dirty on the inside as it was on the outside. The wooden tables that stood along two sides of the room were in need of a good scrub, as was the rubbish littered floor. Dockworkers stood or sat eating chunks of cheese with a slab of bread that had been dunked into their tea while others were puffing on their pipes. Charlotte made her way quickly through the men, many of whom were making remarks to or about her and asked the man who had just finished serving one of the dockworkers, whether she might speak with the owner.

"I am the owner" he snapped, "and can you not see I'm busy?"

"I don't mean to bother you Sir, but please, have you any work I could do?" Charlotte asked. "I will do any work," she continued, "as long as I can earn enough to stay in a lodging house for the winter. I can't bear the thought of having to stay any longer in the rookeries".

The owner of the eating house, an Irish man called Joseph O'Hara looked her up and down. He was tall and fair-haired with smiling blue eyes, a huge moustache and a beard that spread out over his lower face. His left hand was deformed, his fingers curling over each other and into the palm of his hands. He looked about 60 years of age and had lost most of his teeth. He asked her age and on being told began reminiscing about his own daughter, now long dead.

"Our Mary would have been 31 now. Both she and Patrick my son died within a year of each other. It's just me and my wife now" he said.

A dockworker shouting for more tea interrupted his reminiscing any further. After telling Charlotte that she was hired but only for the day, he served the docker while telling Charlotte to hang her cape up and get working. She dearly wanted to give Joseph a hug, but knew it wasn't the proper thing to do. Instead she walked over to him, took the cloth from his gnarled hands and started work.

Joseph thought that Charlotte was going to be a great asset and he could certainly do with a helping hand now and then. More and more men were working at the docks now, most from out of the area, all wanting food. His wife Amy made the parkin cake, suet puddings and his favourite, Irish soda bread at home and Joseph would then pull the food down to the dock side on his old handcart along with cheeses and hams.

Amy was getting frail now and neither of them knew just how long she would be able to carry on cooking the large amounts of food required. After the eatery had closed for the night and the tables, floor and mugs had been thoroughly cleaned Charlotte told Joseph about her life and why she had left her last place of employment.

"I admire your courage girl," said Joseph, "you deserve better in life than you have had so far. We could help each other I suppose, trouble is, I can't afford to pay you a lot."

"I don't mind how little you pay me", exclaimed Charlotte, "Just to have a position, that's all I want."

After paying for her new found lodgings, Charlotte realised that she would still have enough money left to buy a few essentials from time to time. Joseph had told her that she could eat at work, so that saved her some money which she was putting away for new under garments and perhaps a frock...

Joseph began to wonder how he had managed before Charlotte arrived, she worked hard and gone were the sad eyes that he had seen on his first encounter with her. Instead, she had become a woman with a smile that would light even the drabbest London day. The dock workers all had a cheery word for her, which she returned with a smart retort for any that got a little out of line.

Chapter 6

The latest influx of out of area dock workers arrived in the food house on a warm, though windy day in 1807. Among them was a dark haired man with brown eyes and chocolate coloured skin who ordered his food politely and quietly from Charlotte. Taking his cheese and chunk of bread and positioning himself by the door he began to eat whilst staring intently through the grey haze of tobacco smoke at the woman who had just served him. John Mills had met his future wife.

Charlotte knew that John had taken a liking to her so it came as no surprise when, having left work one evening John was waiting for her and walked her to her lodging house. Three times during that year he asked her to marry him. Three times she turned him down. Not because she thought so little of him - she loved the man but felt a deep loyalty to Amy and Joseph. They had treated her with kindness when she had had no one and now treated her as a daughter. The couple were getting on in years now and Charlotte wasn't going to get married and leave them when they needed her most. Marriage for now could wait.

Amy died in 1810 and for a year Charlotte and Joseph ran the business together, cooking in the late evening and serving during the day. Eighteen months later Joseph passed away.

Charlotte tried to keep the business going as the old man had asked, but as each month passed, the takings got less. Although more men were coming into the area, bigger and better eating-houses were opening, and as she didn't have the resources to expand the little business soon closed.

In January 1812 after years of asking, John finally persuaded Charlotte to become his wife. They were both in their mid thirties now and knew that as the years rolled by their hopes of having children were becoming less and less.

So busy had they been, Charlotte making arrangements for their wedding, John working all the hours he could at the Dock that they almost ignored the laboured breathing that John had developed. He had several periods of weakness when work on the dock side had been increasingly difficult for him. At times he was unable to keep up with the other workers, which would irritate them. It was strenuous work and all hands were needed to keep the team going. John seemed much better by the summer of 1812 and he was sure that given time he would be able to work as fast as the others once more.

The wedding dress was of soft muslin, which clung to Charlotte's body, highlighting the contours of her figure. Underneath she wore a satin slip and a small bustle pad to lift the fullness at the back of the dress. The bonnet was of ruche and pleated taffeta with a wide brim that framed Charlotte's tiny face. She had coiled her hair up onto the crown of her head and secured it with a tortoiseshell comb. The rest of her curls fell from under the bonnet like tiny, tight corkscrews. She carried a small circular purse with ribbon drawstrings. Charlotte didn't care that everything she was wearing was old and used, John had said how beautiful she looked and she felt beautiful. They were now man and wife. It was a morning wedding as the law stated and they celebrated with a small wedding breakfast in the taproom of the local tavern along with two friends who had acted as witnesses for them.

After their marriage Charlotte and John rented a large room in a lodging house close to the docks. Their marriage certificate was displayed under a clock that hung on the wall, a custom that some people deemed to bring good luck. The room was very basic and sparsely furnished, but they were happy there.

All too soon summer was gone, replaced by autumn. Leaves started to fall and the air became damp and dismal followed by a really hard winter. The weather was so bad that on February 2nd 1814 part of the Thames was frozen over with a thick blanket of ice. It was there that a frost fair was held and attended by thousands of people from all over the area. John, by this time had sought the help of an apothecary who gave him advice concerning his laboured breathing which had been troubling him again.

"You have asthma or epilepsy of the lungs which is caused by constrictions of the Bronchi, the airways into the lungs. All I can suggest is that it may help if you move away from the fog and foul air of London and take laudanum, a mixture of opium and alcohol," the apothecary explained.

In a letter to his brother who lived in Eastry, Kent, John explained about his ill health and asked that should a position become available in his place of employment that he put his name forward as being available for work.

The good news came by mail coach in May 1814.

Dear Brother,

On the reception of your letter of the 28th and after making the necessary inquiries of my Employer, I report to you this.

An under gardener is required to help in the extensive grounds of one of the large houses in the village. The work entails tending the lawns, pruning fruit trees, weeding and digging the numerous flower beds, sweeping the grounds and any other work that owner of the house requires. The hours of work would be 6.30am until 6pm with one half hour break

a day. There is also a small cottage that could be rented if required. Would you be interested? If so, will you kindly let me know your expected arrival time and I will ensure that everything is in order at the cottage.
Yours respectfully,
Thomas.

John and Charlotte were pleased with the offer and sent a letter of thanks and acceptance back straight away. John, who had been born in Kent, knew the air there was far cleaner than that in London and hoped that perhaps his health would improve.

"The area is made up of small winding lanes", he told Charlotte "which run alongside trickling streams and lush fields with deep green hedgerows, under which primroses and bluebells grow".

They sold their meagre belongings to one of the slop houses - the sale of their few items made enough money for a week's rent for their new home and a little over to buy some second-hand furniture - packed the few clothes they possessed and headed for the country.

Unable to afford the stagecoaches which had opened up the opportunity for travel further a-field, they rode the wagon from London, not as comfortable as the stagecoach but far cheaper and quicker than walking.

The wagon took them as far as Sittingbourne where they alighted at the Red Lion, a coaching inn with stables to the rear accessed via a cobbled alley to the side of the building.

After resting an hour John and Charlotte set off on the last part of their journey, this time on foot. All around them were fields of different coloured grasses, which turned the landscape into a giant patchwork quilt.

As dusk fell, they found a small copse and decided that here was where they would spend the night using their bundle of possessions as pillows. Sharing the copse with them were timid rabbits and squirrels, who were settling down for the night watched over by the glowing amber eyes of the crafty foxes.

A little after daylight broke Charlotte and John were on their way again, they hoped they would be at the cottage by early evening. This wasn't to be, they ached from the journey the day before and their footsteps were slower.

A second night was spent sleeping outside, this time on the outskirts of Canterbury in a ditch under a hedgerow. Both were in need of a wash when they awoke and their clothes had become damp with the early morning dew. On reaching Canterbury they refreshed themselves with a steaming mug of tea bought from a teahouse situated just outside Canterbury Cathedral.

"Can we stay a while longer?" Charlotte pleaded, "I do so want to walk around the grounds of the Cathedral, it is said to have beautiful stained glass windows and magnificent architecture."

"There is no time to linger," said John shaking his head, "we have several more miles to walk yet and I would like to reach Eastry as soon as possible, I have to work go to tomorrow."

After devouring the dry chunks of bread they had brought with their belongings when leaving London, they set off once more towards Eastry, arriving just before midday.

Thomas was waiting for them, clutching the key to their new home, a little cottage fronted by a wooden door, in front of which were two steps. Inside was a small passage with doors leading to the parlour and a tiny scullery.

A narrow staircase led to two bedrooms. The main bedroom was small, the other even smaller. The tiny parlour had a window overlooking the dirt road the other side of which was the big house where John would work. The scullery had a food pantry and an old dresser that John said would scrub up to be quite usable for their crockery.

The following day, with John at his new job Charlotte busied herself sweeping and scrubbing the floors after which she gave the pantry and dresser a good wash. Then she cleaned the windows before going upstairs and starting on the bedrooms. Before long every room was clean and fresh.

Chapter 7

The couple knew nothing about Eastry a small village situated approximately three miles from the town of Sandwich, so once John had returned from work and had eaten, he and Charlotte went to find the village church.

Turning left outside their cottage they walked along, past The Bull Inn and stables. A few minutes later they reached The Cross, turned left down a narrow track until they were in view of the beautiful St Mary's Church with its Norman door and windows. The lower part of the Norman tower dates from late eleventh or early twelfth century; from the top of this tower seventeen other churches can be seen. It was lavishly built by the monks of Christ Church Abbey, Canterbury, complete with a calendar carved into a pillar in the knave which they later learned, told the days on which Easter fell. This is where John, Charlotte and others from the eight hundred people that made up the population of the village would come to worship every week.

Having no furniture, John and Charlotte spent the first days in their new home sitting on the floor during the day and sleeping on it at night. The following Saturday they travelled the two miles to the old town of Sandwich, a small but bustling place where people from most of the hamlets around the area gathered.

With the help of their neighbour who owned a horse and small cart, they were hoping to buy some essential furniture. John however, having made his way to the main street, soon found The Bell Inn and before long was supping ale with his neighbour and some of the local men.

Charlotte made her way along the cobbled streets, looking in the shops and making a mental note of the prices of the furniture they needed. Very soon she had purchased an old bed with a big carved wooden head and footboard. The mattress was badly torn in places but Charlotte found a roll of heavy striped ticking and knew that with time and patience she could repair the mattress and have enough ticking left over to be able to stitch some curtains for the two front facing windows of the cottage.

Her next purchase from the same used furniture shop was a cherry finished washbasin stand complete with a mirror. The bottom shelf was made to hold a pitcher; the upper part for the washbasin and towels and although it was old and stained she knew John could make it presentable again. To complete their bedroom she chose a pitcher and basin, they didn't match and the pitcher had a small chip on the lip, but they were cheap and serviceable and that's all that mattered to Charlotte. For the parlour she chose a panel back settee and an old armchair both roughly covered in brown coloured hide. The scullery would be home to the tiny plank table and the two rickety chairs that completed Charlotte's purchases.

Soon the spring of 1815 arrived and they knew their life was about to change yet again. Charlotte was pregnant. They wondered how they would manage with another mouth to feed but despite their worries, they were happy and looked forward to the birth of their baby. That day arrived on November 12th 1815.

The front bedroom was filled with the hearty cries of Charlotte and John's first born, a girl, whom they named

Rebecca, meaning "bound together". With tight dark curls and skin the colour of chocolate she was a beautiful baby. Like many other women, Charlotte had wanted to give birth in hospital but the closest hospital to Eastry, was the imposing Kent and Canterbury, which had opened in 1793 and supported by a list of wealthy subscribers including the local nobility, gentry and clergy. These people were quite clear as to who should and shouldn't be admitted. Some of the inadmissible cases for in-patients were pregnant women, children under seven years (unless for an operation) and people who were dying or incurable.

Rebecca, who was baptised in Eastry Church on January 1817 grew into a shy, pretty, quietly spoken and very polite child. Everyone in the small village knew and liked her including the Master and his wife at the house where her father was employed. She went to school and was taught not only reading, writing and arithmetic but also simple methods of sewing. Evenings were spent sat in the parlour chatting to her parents about world or country events. The story that fascinated Rebecca most was that of the smuggling that had taken place along the coast at Broadstairs, Kent. Rebecca had sat spellbound as her parents told her about Joss Snelling also known as 'The Broadstairs Smuggler'. He ran his Gang between his cottage in Broadstairs and Joss Bay, one of his favourite landing sites. Her parents spoke of Snelling and his Gang being attacked by Revenue men while in the process of unloading a lugger, "The Lark" Joss Snelling and four of his men escaped by climbing the cliffs, they then shot and killed a Revenue officer who tried to stop their escape across a field. After a search one smuggler was found dead and another dying. Her father said that in all, ten smugglers were killed during the chase and six, (her mother said it was eight) were taken alive and later hanged at Gallows Field in Sandwich. In 1829, Joss Snelling was presented to the future Queen Victoria, being introduced as "the famous Broadstairs smuggler".

By her 13th birthday Rebecca, a bright girl with an enquiring mind had finished her schooling and was looking for employment. This she found with Mr and Mrs Roswell as nursemaid to their four children.

They had a large house with a huge sweeping drive, in Wingham on the outskirts of Canterbury. Rebecca's bedroom, at the top of the house was where she would write to her parents and tell them which day of the month she would be visiting them and on these visits she would listen to the tales and gossip of village life.

Like many of her day, she would also give her parents half of her monthly pay even though she was no longer living at home. She knew that the extra pennies would be spent on food for the table or replacing worn clothing for her mother or father. Her father was still working as a gardener for the people at the big house while her mother was a laundry maid but now only worked a few hours a week. Rebecca knew that there were times when her parents struggled financially and considered it her duty to help them whenever she could. The rest of her weekly wage Rebecca saved, only spending when absolutely necessary.

When not at work or at her parents house, she would wile away the hours looking through the windows of the fashionable clothes shops in Canterbury. One shop in particular was the reason she was saving her money. She had fallen in love with a dress that was draped over a bust in the window. The skirt was full and billowing, the bodice waistline was a deep pointed V. The sleeves were "leg of mutton" and Rebecca thought it quite beautiful. By the time she had saved half the cost of the dress, it had been sold.

Tall and slim with black curly hair, which she piled on top of her head, people told her that she didn't need fancy clothes to look good. She knew she was stared at wherever she went but Rebecca thought that it was because of her colour, she never thought of herself as being what she actually was, a very attractive young woman.

After five years service with her employers in Canterbury, they informed Rebecca and the other household staff that they were going to make their home in London. They felt that there were more opportunities in London for two of their sons who were now coming to the end of their schooling. Rebecca was asked to work for them in London, as they would still require someone to look after the two younger children. She had grown to love the children and took pride in her job but she was unsure about leaving her parents and the area she knew so well. She needn't have worried though her parents were overjoyed that she had the offer of going to London to work; realizing that employment was very scarce in Kent.

"You are extremely lucky to have been given this opportunity", smiled her father, "make the most of what you have been offered, your mother and I are very happy for you."

Seven months later Charlotte didn't look happy as with tears in her eyes, she watched her daughter leave their home in Eastry for her new life in London, knowing that they would only see Rebecca twice a year or whenever she could afford the journey back to Kent.

How she wished that she had been able to give her daughter a Tuareg cross, as was the custom in Niger. The crosses were made of silver and the markings and intricate, geometrical designs translate into "no matter where you go, God and I shall always be with you and protect you". Tuareg parents gave these exquisite crosses to their children when they were about to depart from home as a form of good luck and protection.

Although preferring the peacefulness of Kent, Rebecca soon grew accustomed to life in London. John Macadam was transforming the roads that her parents had once known as muddy pot-holed quagmires. By laying a base of broken stone under a drainable surface, such a difference was made to travel, cutting times spent on the roads by half. Most of the streets were now lit by gaslight and Robert Peel had set up a police force in 1829. So much had changed in the years since her parents had lived in London.

Five years later, the youngest of the Roswell children no longer needed a nurse and with excellent references from Mr. Roswell, Rebecca soon found other employment in Lambeth as a nurse-cum-general-maid. The work was harder than she had been used to in the Roswell household; now as well as tending to the child in her care, she would make fires after carrying in the coal. Clean, wash up, cook and make tea, prepare the beds and carrying hot water to the bedrooms. Her last chore of the day was to check that the windows and doors were locked before retiring to her room. She dearly wanted to go home for a while, she had only seen her parents a few times since leaving Kent but knew that she would never find permanent employment there.

On the occasions she had travelled home she had given her parents a few coins to ease the burden of their every day living. Her mother who was now in her mid sixties, was finding it difficult to work the long hours as she had in the past.

This was Rebecca's life, living and working in Lambeth, saving as much as she could of her wages and spending two weekends a year in Kent to be with her parents. Her social life consisted of going to dances with friends or sitting in the park chatting. She had many male admirers, some of whom had tried really hard to have Rebecca walk out with them. She had once spent an evening with an admirer but, after overhearing him telling his friends that he was only with her because he had never lain down with a black woman before, she left and hadn't had a male friend since.

She soon grew to like the area which was becoming well known for its pear trees, vineyards and public gardens where

London inhabitants could find entertainment and refreshment in a rural surrounding. The green land of Lambeth was made good use of with large open spaces used for walking and sometimes for duck hunting while customers of a local tavern could watch their dinner being caught for them in the brooks and ponds.

Chapter 8

Hundreds of miles from London lies Sierra Leone (see-air-uh lee-ohn), a small country on the west coast ("hump") of Africa with grassy savannas in the north, mountains in the east and mangrove swamps along the coast. Varieties of mahogany, palm and teak trees made up the dense forests in the southeast. In the northern grasslands, people reared cattle and grew plants including rice, yam and vegetables. People in the coastal area became fishermen and they traded the fish with the people living further inland.

Throughout the course of the slave trade, millions of Africans became involuntary immigrants to other countries.

Hundreds of black Loyalists who had served in the British forces flocked to London after the American Revolution in 1783 hoping to gain the freedom they had been promised. They acquired their freedom and joined hundreds of free Africans already living in England· Once in the UK, Africans at that time were banned from learning any trade imposed by a 1731 law, which prevented them from finding paid employment. In order to survive many turned to begging.

On 27th February 1787 nearly 270 of the poorest black men, women and children, 20 white women that were married to black men, four white children and five white women wanting to be married, were aboard two ships lying at Motherbank which forms the northern boundary of the parish of Wooton on the Isle of Wight.

These poor blacks and their women who, some said, were common prostitutes were going to the colony of Sierra Leone. They thought it would be a better life than the one they had in Great Britain. Some of the surnames of the coloured people were: Adams, Hill, Green, Simpson and Banks. Many did not reach Sierra Leone having died of fever and disease. Sailing with them were skilled white men including a Doctor, a Parish Sexton, a Bricklayer and a Carpenter.

The journey took approximately seven weeks and some 60 plus settlers died on route. For those who did survive, the sight of the high mountains some distance from Sierra Leone was a moment of great joy. Freetown became a fair sized and novel community, made up of the arrival of both blacks and whites of Great Britain and the Africans from Nova Scotia.

The slave trade was abolished in the 1800s and the British put great effort into trying to wipe out slavery and the slave trade in Africa.

Freetown, the capital, was taken over by the British government in early 1808, who used it as a naval base for antislavery patrols. As the 1880's approached, it appeared that West Africa was completely dominated by Britain.

The families of some of the African chieftains gained from British rule, they wore British clothes, adopted the English language and some were educated in Britain. Many took up posts in the civil service in West Africa the senior posts though were always taken by British officials.

For the more ordinary West Africans however, British rule brought enormous changes of a very different sort to their everyday lives. A system of owning, buying and selling land, was one brought in by the British which meant many Africans had to pay rent. Now instead of growing crops like cocoa or rubber to buy food, they had to grow crops to sell in order to be able to pay those rents. The African traditional crafts that had been handed down over many centuries were all but destroyed by competition from goods produced in British factories.

It was here in Sierra Leone in 1816 that Sarah squatted on the beaten earthed floor of the thatched mud hut that she shared with her husband Samuel. All day she had had stomach pains. Perspiring heavily and trying to cool herself, Sarah took a piece of cloth and dipped it into the wooden bowl of water and pushing her thick black curly hair back as far as she could, she placed the cloth on her forehead. The coolness which lasted just a few minutes was so welcome, she squatted a while longer, then rose and wandered to the front of the hut. In the distance, she could see the large muscular frame of Samuel her husband, 6ft 1ins tall, ebony skin, hair the colour of coal. She called to him and he smiled as he turned towards her, knowing that it would soon be time for their baby's birth.

Some time later, Samuel, on hearing the unmistakable cries of his first born, strode proudly into the hut. Sarah was sitting on the earth floor. In her arms she was cradling their son. Taking him from his mother Samuel gently touched his son's cheek and seven days later, named him Caesar, which means practical, responsible, determined, self-reliant, and capable.

Since African names have a clear meaning, Samuel knew that by naming his son thus, it would have a huge significance on Caesar as he grew up. He also knew that the child's birth, growing up, his marriage and death would all be celebrated with centuries old traditions.

Caeser's birth was the signal for huge rejoicing, first though, there would be a period of waiting to make sure the baby was healthy and strong before the celebrations began. Caesar was born into a home where traditions and customs were taught. Respect and obedience instilled through guidance rather than discipline and the history of his ancestors listened to and learnt by heart.

Home for this family was close to the base of a British naval squadron who searched various vessels to see if they were carrying slaves. Caesar was seven years old when he witnessed such an event. A Portuguese ship was intercepted in April 1822, by the British anti-slavery patrols and thousands of uprooted, disorientated people from inland Africa were put ashore in Sierra Leone.

In 1826, the Honourable House of Commons ordered a paper on the Requisitions for articles for Liberated Africans.

This was printed in March of that year and included such things as:

15000 yards of check for shirts = £671 17s 6d.

Duck Frocks for men and boys = £1375.

Braces, large size shoes, check linen for dresses as well as 200 Great Coats for the Masters = £1924 10s

Felling axes, pick axes, hoes, hatchets, and handsaws, together with other tools for clearing land and erecting buildings came to a total of well over £726.

Caesar was 12 years old when the Church Missionary Society established Fourah Bay College, its aim was to develop

Christian leadership for Africa. This college was to eventually offer the first university education in West Africa. Christianity was taught to the natives in an effort to cleanse them.

One African was said to have told his children many years later:

"When the white people came they had Bibles and we had land. They taught us to pray with our eyes closed. When they had finished, they had the land and we had the Bibles".

Almost every year Caesar witnessed the damage the rainy season would bring to the land, lashing winds, rain falling in torrents and loud thunder that would echo from the mountains causing a frightening noise. Many times his parents' hut had been badly damaged and when the weather broke and the blue skies returned, the task of rebuilding and re-thatching would begin.

His move from childhood to adulthood was carefully marked and charted and when he reached the age of thirteen it was time for the initiation ritual .

Although frightened, Caesar understood that this was the tribal way of his people. As part of the ritual which serves as a symbol of initiation into adulthood, he and another twenty boys were isolated from their village. For three months they lived in a secret camp within a forest where they received training and education in the spiritual beliefs and practices of their ethnic group. They were also taught the responsibilities they would bear as adult members of their society. Once the initiation period was over, they were marched back into the village and greeted with much celebration, dance and a special feast held in their honour. Caesar returned to his village, a thirteen year old man with the right to now take a wife.

By 1831 Samuel worked as a cook, Sarah a market woman. Caesar had long left home and was a servant to one of the many white families that were living in Freetown. He helped in the kitchens, menial jobs to start with, but two years later, with the death by fever of the head cook, Caesar was placed in charge of the kitchen and the cooking. He had no trouble adapting to his new job, from an early age he had watched and listened to his father and Samuel was one of the best cooks around. Knowing that he was one of the lucky few to have found employment Caesar carried out his duties perfectly and his master spoke very highly of him, but Caesar had a true passion of the sea and the ships that sailed on her. His free time would be spent down by the dock wondering which lands the ships with their huge sails and tall masts were sailing to.

Chapter 9

The years went by and in 1839 Caesar heard talk of other work being offered. Many men from West Africa possessed skills of seamanship for which Europeans were prepared to pay a fee. These men would pour forth each day to work at sea as porters, boatmen and cooks. Some would be required for just one voyage others would be employed on a more permanent basis. Whenever he could slip away from his work, Caesar would line up with the other men willing the Master of whatever ship was looking for workers, to pick him.

In January 1840 his perseverance was rewarded, he was picked to be the cook on a ship bound for Great Britain. Detailed contracts between seamen and employers had become law in 1835.

So it was that Caesar was asked to give his age where he resided and whether he had been on a previous ship. The date of joining and leaving this ship would be noted in the crew agreement along with any illness or disciplinary action that related to him. Joining him aboard ship were thirteen other men including the Master, Mate, Boatman and Carpenter. Able Seamen made up the rest of the crew. Provisions would be allocated to provide 1lb of bread per day, with beef on Saturday Sunday Tuesday and Thursday. Pork would be served on Monday Wednesday and Fridays as well as ¼ oz tea daily plus three quarts of water. The salary of £2.5s would be paid in advance. Caesar signed his contract with an X.

His mother was anxious, his father pleased.

"Once he arrives in that foreign land what will he encounter? Our own parent's returned to West Africa from London because of the hardship and poverty they had endured there," wailed Sarah. "You know life was so hard for them that they were known as the London Poor, will life there be any better now? Things are hard here in our own country, but at least we are together."

"Hush woman," replied Samuel, "Caesar has no guaranteed long term employment here. His position of cook will only last until the white missionary family leave for their homeland. It's time for us to let him go."

Five days later, Sarah and Samuel stood and watched as their first-born disappeared below the decks of the ship. Samuel returned immediately to his work but Sarah stood barefoot by the dock side until the ship was just a speck on the horizon. Their son was now in charge his own destiny.

Below decks, Caesar familiarized himself with the layout of the galley and mess, where he would spend his time whilst on board, making sure every meal was properly cooked and served correctly. If he was to have a future as a ship's steward he would have to ensure from the start that everything was perfect. His own, as well as the other crew members' personal space on board was very limited, his room below decks was poorly ventilated and just big enough to lay down in.

On the second day a storm broke and what a storm it was, with waves appearing as if they were rolling liquid hills. Kettles, cooking pots and cans were tossed back and forth as the wind howled and waves hit the side of the ship tossing it from side to side. The bow lifted on the huge rolling waves and as it descended into the dark void that the passing wave had left, the stern lifted high into the air, while the whole ship made a horrendous noise. Spray from the waves drenched the deck and everything on it. As the huge ship dipped and then rose again and again, Caesar felt sicker than he had ever done before, but he couldn't let it be known that he felt so awful, that would make him appear weak and no-one hired a weak man. As the bile rose up into his throat with every movement of the ship, he had carried on with his duties. At last it was over and the following morning the weather was calm and pleasant.

Through a haze of fine drizzle, which made every building look grey and dull, his first glimpse of London was something that Caesar would never forget. He wondered how he would ever find his way around without becoming lost; he hadn't realised that there would be so many people, houses and streets in one place. Here and there men were going about their daily chores, others just sitting near the dock side idly chatting. Men with tired eyes, torn coats and worn shoes rushed to the side of the docks, hoping as he had once hoped that they would be picked for work. Women with their bright red lips and rouged cheeks, smelling of cheap cologne were standing close to the docks, teenagers, middle aged women and some in their sixties. Some were quite beautiful, others toothless hags. They smiled sweetly at the sailors who had left the ships and were making their way to the nearest tavern, hoping to relieve them of some of their hard earned pay in exchange for a "good time".

Children too, were milling around the dock side begging for a few coppers, children with matted hair, dirty faces and equally dirty clothes. Some had been climbers (chimney sweeps) who had been too frightened to go up another chimney and had run away from their master. Others were orphaned or just abandoned, home for these poor children were the cold hard streets. He wished he could help in some way but Caesar knew he must find a place to stay and would need all of his hard earned wages just for that. Walking along the road with his worldly possessions wrapped in brown paper and tied with string, he thought how lucky he was to have work and from that work the pleasure of knowing that he could buy something to eat and be able to sleep in a dry comfortable place.

Four months later after a voyage to Demerara and back, Caesar was laid off. With a small amount of money saved from his wages but little hope of finding other employment other than at the docks he spent his days walking from ship to ship pleading for a work. Nights were spent on any floor or dirty mattress in what ever lodging house had a vacancy. Once a week he took his clothes to an old washer woman Mrs Maynard who rented a couple of rooms at number 9, three doors away from where he was lodging. She charged just a few coppers for what she called a full week's wash. A weekly wash according to her rule was no more that one shirt, one pair of trousers and two undergarments. She worked hard and was well known and much liked by the local people.

Caesar was waiting at number 9 to collect his wash a few weeks later when a horse and carriage drew level with him. The occupant a tall bearded man with clear blue eyes, in his early seventies beckoned Caesar and asked that he may have a word.

"My name is Mr. Langdon," he explained, "and I'm looking for a general servant-cum-gardener for my smallholding, one who would be able to start work immediately. I'm moving home shortly, my present one being too large for me since my wife passed away. I know Mrs Maynard very well as she had been in my employ years ago leaving only when she became pregnant with her first child. I couldn't have kept her on, my house wasn't a suitable place for children, and," he said to Caesar with a wry grin, "I couldn't abide children back then, nothing but little perishers I thought. Anyway, as I was saying, this morning, I asked Mrs Maynard whether she knew any trustworthy chaps, suitable for a position in my house.

She described you young man and told me that if I wished to speak to you, you would be at her house to collect your wash when the clock struck 4pm. Should you be interested in the position, the rules I enforce are no lying, no thieving and no laziness."

Although Caesar didn't particularly like the thought of being a servant he knew that he was lucky to be offered this position with such a kindly old gent. Many other people were unemployed and would love a position like this, parents with children dying from measles, mumps, polio and hunger. Parents too poor to buy even basic medicines living in appalling conditions with little or nothing to eat , and so he presented himself at the house in Greenford two weeks later.

Chapter 10

In Saxon times Greenford was know as Grenanforda, a tiny village with the River Brent and Paddington Canal flowing through it and had been mentioned three times in the Doomsday book. At that time it listed just nine villagers, three cottages, seven smallholders, a Frenchman and six slaves. The church was an ancient building of flint, which Mr. Langdon told Caesar as they passed by, was believed to be from the 15th Century. The area was mostly agricultural and the population very small.

Mr. Langdon's medium sized, very untidy house lay on the outskirts of the village. In the front parlour the expensive furniture including the window seat and rosewood sofa, appeared to dwarf the room as did the mahogany table and chairs in the dining room.

"Items" Mr. Langdon explained "purchased by my wife when we lived in the larger house and I have no intention of exchanging them for anything smaller". Caesar, unable to think of anything to say just nodded in agreement.

Rows of pots and pans complete with dust and particles of food were stacked on the open back oak dresser in the scullery. Clearly Mr. Langdon had trouble looking after himself thought Caesar, as he noticed the dirty dishes that had been left on the table. Upstairs were three bedrooms, the larger of which seemed to be dominated by an enormous bed. Against one wall stood a mahogany four-door robe with drawers under and a matching tallboy. Next door was a smaller room that was used as a study, housing a leather topped Davenport desk and a hide-covered library chair.

The smallest of the rooms at the rear of the house, was Caesar's. The furniture had seen better days but the bed in cast iron with a decorative head and a thick mattress was quite comfortable. An old wooden elbow chair with the upholstery in need of repair and a two door wardrobe with hanging space on one side and drawers on the other completed the furnishings.

The smallholding which Mr. Langdon had bought and wanted cultivated was half an hours walk from the house. The produce from the smallholding would provide food to sell to the local people and sustain both him and Caesar who would divide his working hours between both the house and the smallholding.

Happy months were spent with both master and servant getting to know each other. Caesar respected the old man who was kind and considerate to him. The old man spoke to him in a civil manner, never asked too much of him just asked that he did his job. In turn, Mr. Langdon had grown quite fond of the strapping Negro whose work he could not fault and whose manners were impeccable. Come evening time when the weather was fine they would sit together on old chairs by the doorstep, Caesar listening to his master reminiscing. He spoke of his wife and how he had cared for her in her final months and how much he missed her, and went into details of his work as an ink maker and printer, work he had done from a young man until four years previously when his eyesight had started to fail.

Caesar then told his master of his home and his life and family in Sierra Leone. The look of horror on his master's face when he told him of the African ritual into manhood made him want to laugh but of course, he didn't. Locals thought the old man slightly mad to be on such friendly terms with a servant and a black servant at that. Mr. Langdon though had always treated people as he himself would have wanted to be treated had their roles been reversed and always remembered his own fathers words, "as good as a master is, so are his servants."

In the spring of 1841 the smallholding was bursting into life with the first of the year's crop. While Caesar went about his work, removing the endless weeds that were growing faster than the plants, his master chatted amiably to him and whilst doing so asked "Have you ever had a lady friend, someone to walk out with?"

Caesar kept on hoeing and with a laugh his master slapped him on the back saying,

"I do declare you haven't! Well, well it's time you found one."

A few days later the mailman stopped outside the house and handed Mr. Langdon a letter. After the two men had exchanged pleasantries the mailman got back on the coach and went on his way. Caesar was in the scullery setting the tray for his master's mid morning tea. The teapot, milk jug and sugar bowl were no longer discoloured, he had spent hours cleaning all the silver and could see his face in every piece. With each room scrubbed and tidied the house looked very different to when he had first arrived. Fire hearths were gleaming, windows shone and everything was in its place.

When he reached the parlour with the tea tray, Mr. Langdon was sitting by the hearth reading his letter.

"It is," he told Caesar, "from my sister Mrs Peters who lives in Lambeth. Her granddaughter is getting married and I of course, have been invited. The wedding feast will be held at my sister's house, outside on the lawns, weather permitting. As there are nearly one hundred people invited, she has asked me if I might permit you to work in the kitchens with her own staff. It would save the family having to hire another pair of hands for the day and she knew that her neighbours would be quite impressed that she had another black servant, as they have become very fashionable of late."

"Well my man," he said to Caesar, "shall we do this for my rather snooty but likable sister?"

The bride's family were well known for being very successful business people and the guest list consisted entirely of the very upper classes which included aristocrats and nobility. Some guests, elegantly dressed in luxurious clothes were mingling on the lawn drinking fine wines from exquisite glasses and eating from the finest of china. Other groups were admiring the extensive gardens whilst sheltering from the June sun under the canopy formed by the branches of two old oak trees.

Downstairs in the kitchen Caesar and the staff of the house were hard at work, arranging more food onto elaborately decorated silver serving trays before carrying them into the gardens to the waiting guests. He had felt rather awkward at first, never having attended anything as grand as this and to make matters worse, a slim dark skinned girl had caught his eye as soon as he had been shown into the kitchens and he couldn't get her out of his mind. Rebecca had also noticed Caesar, as had all of the other female staff from the moment he had stepped down from Mr. Langdon's carriage. As staff discreetly walked the gardens to refill or collect empty wine glasses, Rebecca made it her business to keep Caesar within her sight so she could walk back to the kitchens with him, an act that hadn't escaped the watchful eyes of Mr. Langdon.

It was 8.30am before Mr. Langdon rose the next morning, complaining to Caesar that he had a headache to end all headaches caused by too much wine the day before and an extremely late night. The headache didn't stop him ribbing Caesar unmercifully about the young girl who had taken an obvious liking to him. Asked when he was going to ask her to walk out with him. Caesar said nothing. He had already done just that.

Chapter 11

Caesar and Rebecca spent the little free time they had in each others company, each telling the other of their parents and what life had been like for them in the past.

On sunny days they went to one of the many ponds in the Lambeth area and spent idle afternoons feeding the ducks or watching young children play five stones or hoops. Other times were spent with two friends Sarah Good and Henry Smith who were also servants and the four of them would make their way to one of the many coffee houses that were becoming increasingly popular. There they would sit and chat about the highlights of their week, politics or the good old British weather.

Certain coffee houses became associated with different political viewpoints or kinds of commercial activity. It was in one of these coffee houses called New Jonathan's that merchant entrepreneurs gathered and formed the early London Stock Exchange.

As the days grew shorter and summer made way for autumn, Caesar and Rebecca began discussing their future as a couple. They both loved each other but knew that they could not afford a home of their own no matter how small. They decided that for the time being at least they would continue as they were, meeting whenever they could.

One cold November day, Rebecca accompanied by Caesar travelled to Eastry. They would only be able to stay an hour or two, but she wanted her parents approval of the man she hoped to marry one day and to give them the Christmas gifts she had bought them. There was a snuffbox with a small shield in the centre for her father and for her mother a tiny pincushion. After having eaten home made bread between which lay thick slices of ham and caught up on all the London gossip they said their goodbyes and Mr and Mrs Mills watched as their daughter and Caesar left for the return journey. Both agreed Rebecca could not do better for a husband.

Christmas came in a flurry of snow, Mr. Langdon spent it with his sister and her family, Caesar of course went with him, serving his employer there as he did in his own house. The hosts and guests, of whom there were many, joined in charades, dancing, games, fireworks, magic lantern shows and piano sing songs with all of them making their own lively entertainment. Their performances were amateur, but they entered into the spirit of the family party with great enthusiasm. When the last of the freshly washed cutlery, crockery, cut glass bowls and crystal wine glasses were neatly replaced onto the dressers and the remains of the uneaten food carefully covered with muslin, Caesar gave Rebecca her present. Nestling in a royal blue jewellery roll was a fine gold chain.

"Thank you," she said, "it is just exquisite."

Her present to Caesar was an open-faced pocket watch.

"It's not a new one," she explained "for I still send money to my parents and a new watch was more than I could afford, but I do hope you like it."

Caesar was thrilled and thought her the most thoughtful and beautiful person he had ever met and kissed her cheek. The rest of the staff were clapping and cheering when Mr.

Langdon came into the kitchen and asked what all the noise was for, the staff were only too eager to tell. The old man looked at Caesar, gave him a wink and went to his bedroom, grinning.

Boxing Day, the feast of St. Stephen and the day that alms boxes at every English church were opened and the contents distributed to the poor. This was also the day that servants traditionally got the whole day off to celebrate with their families, although Mr. Langdon had asked that Caesar might find time to bed his and his sister's horses down at the end of the day. With the whole day and most of the evening to themselves Caesar and Rebecca went to watch Ira Aldridge who had come to Britain in 1825. Together with their friends Sarah and Henry they had saved hard all year for this event, both couples so looking forward to doing something different. Ira had toured Britain for many years starring in productions such as Macbeth and Othello to packed houses in and around London but had never made it in the prestigious Covent Garden theatres, due mainly to the racism of the London press.

For Rebecca and Caesar, Boxing Day 1841 was also the day that they became a couple. After a day of sitting close together and holding hands in the theatre, they then went for a stroll through one of the nearby parks. The sky was a grey blue colour and the icy wind bore a promise of more snow as they reached the home of Mrs Peters. Rebecca pulled her cloak closer to her, how glad she was of this garment in chilly weather. Caesar asked whether Rebecca would like to sit a while in the warmth of the stables while he did the one task that had been asked of him, it was his day off but he would never let his master down. Animals require attention seven days a week and he was quite willing to make sure that all was well with the horses. Inside the stables, Rebecca removed her cloak and started to help cleaning the manure from the floor, and was about to lay fresh bedding down for the horses. With her arms full of straw she could not have stopped Caesar removing her bonnet even if she had wished to. Her thick, shiny hair was parted in the centre, with ringlets at the crown and sides, her eyes shone brightly in the glow of the lamp that was hanging on the stable door.

His large hands held her tiny face as he bent to kiss her. Afterwards, they lay in each other's arms listening to the wind rushing in beneath the stable door, Rebecca shivered and Caesar held her closer whilst wrapping her in his topcoat. In the distance the church clock struck 10 o'clock.

They adjusted their clothes, gently picked all traces of straw from each others hair, quietly closed the stable door and made their way to the back of the house. Once there, they had one final kiss before opening the door and letting themselves in through the servants entrance.

Mr Langdon and Caesar were back home with the Christmas festivities still fresh in their minds and talk often reverting to what a jolly time they had all had. The following Wednesday, Caesar carried his masters tray with a pot of tea and two boiled eggs up to his bedroom.

They had planned to go to the smallholding and were going to make an early start. Much work needed to be done if the crops were to be plentiful. Caesar pulled the drapes to allow a little daylight into the room and could tell immediately that Mr. Langdon was not at all well. His face was grey and he was perspiring profusely, he told Caesar that he felt awful and didn't feel like eating breakfast but needed a doctor. Having run for nearly a mile Caesar stood breathless, knocking on Dr Jones's door.

A short elderly man with small ferret-like eyes staring out from a face that was almost lost in side-whiskers, moustache and beard, Dr Jones had trained at St Bartholomew's Hospital. Like most medical pupils and first year students he had bound himself to a teacher in order to gain an apprenticeship. Most of his medical education was received by attending the wards and following Surgeons as they went about their work, known some time later as "walking the wards". Mr. Jones had left the hospital after a few years, preferring instead to live and work in a smaller community.

"The man has pneumonia," he explained to Caesar as he left Mr. Langdon's house, "he must remain in bed for some time, I have left my bill for attending him on the table by his bed. I shall call later to see how he is."

The following day after ensuring that his employer was comfortable, his loyal companion walked down to the smallholding. There was much work to be done even at this time of the year. The frost that had covered the ground at 4.30 that morning had long since gone. Now was a good time to plant the shallots. The hours flew by and at 1pm Caesar went back to the house and served his master the vegetable broth that he had made the evening before. After washing Mr. Langdon's hands and face, plumping up his pillows and washing the soup bowl and spoon he made his way back to the smallholding with his master's instructions firmly in his mind.

Caesar had never pruned a fruit tree before but had listened intently to what the old man had told him. First he removed the low branches that prevented him from working underneath the tree, then climbing up into the tree he began to thin out the really high branches. This task completed, he began to thin out the centre branches which would make the next crop of apples larger in size. At last the pruning was complete. Checking the rest of the allotment before returning to the house for the evening Caesar noticed that the autumn sown broad beans were looking just about right having broken through the soil and grown an inch or two. Unfortunately a few of them were already providing a meal for some hungry animal that, having dug them up had feasted on them.

Mr. Langdon never fully recovered from the bout of pneumonia, which left him weak and easily tired, but two months later he went to the smallholding. Caesar could see that just pottering around trying to pull a few weeds was too strenuous for the old man and on returning home, settled his master into bed and called for the doctor again. On entering the bedroom it was obvious that the old man had suffered a stroke but, stubborn as he was refused to be hospitalized.

"I will," he told the doctor, "have daily house calls from you, for which I will pay you extremely well and Caesar can make me as comfortable here in my own home as I would be in hospital".

The stroke left Mr. Langdon with a limp in his left leg and an arm that hung loosely by his side, more than ever he came to rely on Caesar who in turn was only too pleased to do anything to help this kind considerate gentleman.

Arrangements were made that Mrs Peters would come to stay at Greenford every Tuesday morning and return to Lambeth at 6pm the following day in order to look after her brother. This allowed Caesar time to harvest the produce from the smallholding and sell it to the local people, thus ensuring that money was still coming into the household. Rebecca accompanied her Mistress and helped Caesar in the kitchen on the Tuesday evenings, preparing meals for the following day. This done, Rebecca and Caesar would enjoy an hour or so down by the river. Sitting on the bank Rebecca would slip her arm through his and they would sit and dream of all the things they would like to do. Their dream was that one day they would be married and have a home of their own, for now though they settled for the precious moments snatched on Tuesday evenings after the household chores were finished.

One evening in October 1842 as they were about to walk back from the river, Rebecca buried her head in her hands and wept as if her heart would break. Caesar had noticed a change in her weeks before and had an idea what was wrong. Now they had more problems than they knew how to cope with. If Rebecca told her Mistress she would surely lose her job, if Caesar told Mr. Langdon he too would be without employment. They decided to say nothing to anyone and agreed that they would stay in work for as long as they were able to enable them to save all they could for the birth of their baby.

As the months past Rebecca would pull her corsets tighter and hope that no one would notice her ever-expanding stomach. In the early months she would rise an hour earlier, so that the waves of nausea bought on by morning sickness had passed before she tended to her Mistresses needs. Each month she and Caesar would take their wages and hunt the used clothing shops or market stalls for baby clothes, which Rebecca would hide on top of the cupboard in her room.

December and Christmas of 1842 came and went, Mr. Langdon's health had shown no signs of improvement over the year. There were days when he just stayed in his bedroom sometimes propped up in the bed, other times he sat in the hide covered library chair that Caesar had bought in from the other bedroom. It was in January of the following year when unannounced, Mr. Langdon's sister arrived at his house, stony faced with a very red eyed Rebecca trailing behind her.

"Caesar is a very loyal, sincere servant," Mr Langdon told his sister, "He knows my ways, my likes and dislikes, my moods and tempers. I really don't want to lose him, however, I do not want a child in this house."

"To lose Rebecca would be foolish also," his sister mused, "who else would work as long and as hard as she does for the wage that she receives. Being pregnant hasn't affected her work and providing she doesn't let the baby interfere with her duties after it is born and she keeps it below stairs at all times, she can continue with her employment with me. I must say though that these arrangements go against everything that I stand for, to have a woman employed in my house who is about to give birth to a bastard child, and a coloured one at that. The thought makes me feel quite faint. I insist that Rebecca and Caesar marry as soon as possible."

Wagging her finger in Rebecca's face she shouted "think yourself very, very lucky indeed young lady," then turning on her heel Mrs Peters glared at Caesar and swept out of the house, shouting at Rebecca to hurry up and follow her.

Caesar had every intention of marrying Rebecca, his child would never be referred to as a bastard. He knew what an awful life these children and their mothers had. They were the sole responsibility of their mothers and if the mothers of these children were unable to support themselves and their offspring, they would be put into the workhouse.

The following week, Caesar had prepared the dinner tray for Mr. Langdon having made him a broccoli and potato casserole, followed, should he fancy it by a piece of his favourite lemon gingerbread cake. An hour later, when the bell from his master's bedroom rang in the kitchen, Caesar returned to fetch the empty tray.

"Plump my pillows and help me back into bed would you?" asked Mr Langdon, "then to listen to what I have to say. The local church, according to my sister, has refused to conduct the marriage between yourself and Rebecca. Some of the local people are still very prejudiced. Unfortunately the majority of these are landed gentry who pour large amounts of money into the church funds."

For the first time in his life Caesar felt intense rage. He was not frowned upon when it came to digging the crops from the ground in order that these self-righteous people could then send their servants to buy the produce. None of them were prejudiced when it came to him looking after one of their own race, which he had done in a dignified and loyal manner. Looking at Caesar's proud, but angry looking face Mr. Langdon went on,

"Through the friends I made and kept in touch with whilst working in the printing business, I am sure that there is a way for the marriage to take place in St Brides in Fleet Street. There would of course be certain criteria to meet and extra payments be made to the appropriate people but I will see what I can do."

"Thank you Sir, I really am most grateful," replied Caesar.

By the first week in February, the wedding was arranged and Mr. Langdon gave the couple a brief history of the church they were to marry in. St. Brides had a very impressive tower from which hung one of London's four curfew bells, the law at one time being, after the bell had tolled "No man shall be so daring as to go wandering about the city unless he be a man of good repute, with reasonable cause and with light."

"Of course," Mr Langdon went on, "after the Great Fire of London, St Brides was rebuilt by Christopher Wren. It was this church that hundreds of weeping people flocked to as the death carts trundled past when over 2000 men women and children died of the plague in 1665. In 1764 lightning struck the church steeple which was said to be Wren's tallest reducing the height by 8ft. The history of the church goes back much further though, as there has been a place of worship on the site since before Roman times. "

The church was every bit as beautiful as Mr. Langdon had described it and on Wednesday 1st March 1843, the couple walked the length of the spectacular aisle and were greeted by the Vicar, Mr. Jones.

The shape of Rebecca's dress was very much the fashion of previous years having been worn at one time by Mrs Peters and then used for a ball gown by her eldest daughter. Rebecca had altered the frock which was far too long, the material from the bottom she had inserted down both sides of the nipped-in low waist to accommodate her now swollen stomach. The full skirt of the frock almost touched the ground and the dropped shoulders with tight sleeves fitted her perfectly.

The material was of striped silk in a very delicate shade of blue. On her head she wore a wide brimmed bonnet in a contrasting shade of blue, with feather trimmings. Her hands, in which she carried a small bible, were encased in cream gloves the colour being a very near match to her low heeled shoes which she had borrowed from Sarah.

Standing beside her was Caesar in his dark trousers and double-breasted tailcoat, with its collar, high at the back and low at the front. With Sarah Good and Henry Smith as their witnesses, they were ready to take their vows and be pronounced man and wife.

How different Caesar's marriage was to the marriages of his friends and relatives in Sierra Leone where things were far more complicated. There if a girl accepted her husband-to-be after his initial approach, he sent his head wife (if he is already married) or female member of his family to the parents of the girl with a present of money. The money was then divided between the girls family. The Father received half, the eldest natural uncle, one quarter and the bride's brother, one quarter. If the girl was illegitimate then the mother claimed all of the money.

Rebecca's parents didn't attend the wedding, it being too expensive and the long journey one they could not undertake. They had written to them, sending them all good wishes for their future happiness and enclosing a small amount of money. Charlotte also told them of the saying about marrying in March which says:

"If you wed when March winds do blow, more sorrow than joy both you'll know."

Like most men, John thought it was a load of nonsense, but with the passing of the years the saying became very true for Rebecca and Caesar.

Chapter 12

Life for the couple changed very little after their marriage. Caesar continued to work for Mr. Langdon, Rebecca still worked for his sister. Now however when they had days or an evening off, they would spend it together quite openly. March turned to April, the month that people looked forward to for many reasons; the heralding of the beginning of spring, the start of longer evenings and the sun climbing higher in the sky. Together they watched as plants and hedgerows burst into growth and the birds started their annual courtship. They were looking forward to the birth of their baby and the long days of the promised summer to come. April though, can bring all types of weather from sunshine to thunder to mild muggy and drizzly days.

It was on a foggy morning just two months after their marriage that a daughter was born to Caesar and Rebecca. She was delivered in Rebecca's bedroom with the help of Sarah and another servant who promptly whisked the baby to the side of the room where a bowl, pitcher of water and clean rags had been placed when Rebecca had had her first contraction. They named the baby Charlotte Eliza and totally adored her.

Life after the birth of Charlotte was extremely hard especially for Rebecca who had to keep the Peters household happy and her baby quiet. Weather permitting she would lay Charlotte in her baby carriage and wheel her into the back yard but after five months when September came and the air was cooler; she had no option but to let the baby stay in the scullery with her. There were days when Mrs Peters would rant at Rebecca about her "screaming brat" and tell her that it was the worse thing she could have done to allow her to stay on, she should have sent her packing as soon as she became pregnant. These were times when, come nightfall, Rebecca would go to her room, crawl into her bed totally exhausted and cry for her husband.

Meanwhile Caesar was still looking after the smallholding and caring for Mr. Langdon, whose health had not improved at all despite extra medication and the wholesome food Caesar cooked for him. Some days he would sit outside in his invalid carriage, on better days he would potter around the house or back yard leaning heavily on two walking sticks. He had been reduced to having to ask for help with his feeding and afterwards to be taken to attend his ablutions. Caesar hated to see him like this.

The funeral of Mr. Langdon, which was lavish in the extreme took place in May 1846 and was attended by most of the local people. Upper class stood nearly but not quite, side-by-side with the lower class, all of them saying their goodbyes to a respected gentleman. His coffin was intricately carved and decorated with gilding, and the horses pulling the funeral carriage were adorned with black ostrich plumes. Walking with his family and friends were the professional mourners (called 'mutes') looking sad and melancholy.

Mrs Peters moved into her brother's house after the funeral, with the intention of winding up his affairs and selling the house and smallholding.

"You realise that you will then be homeless and without a job," she spat at Caesar.

"Might you have work for me at your home?" He asked Mrs Peters.

The answer was a resounding "no".

Rebecca had to now provide for their child and give Caesar money for the rent on the dingy basement room he had found. No matter how careful she was with her wage the money didn't go far. Each mealtime after feeding Charlotte, she would halve whatever food was left and give it to Caesar when he called to see her and his daughter in the evening. She extended the wear of some of Charlotte's clothes by un-picking the back seams and sewing in pieces of cleaning rags. Her own clothes were in need of replacing but that was a luxury she just couldn't afford.

Several weeks later Mr. Langdon's will was read, the last bequeath was, "To my trusted, loyal and hardworking servant Caesar Fitzgerald, I leave , with my heartfelt gratitude for all that you have been to me, the sum of £15."

Rebecca and Caesar were astonished at the kindness of Mr. Langdon. They had never been treated so well and thought things would now be better for them. Caesar spoke of buying their baby some clothes and a new frock for Rebecca. He could now pay the rent on his room without having to take any of his wife's money. Three days later a letter arrived from Eastry that changed their lives again.

Rebecca's mother was ill; for several months she had had trouble with her breathing and lately had been passing out. The letter asked Rebecca to come to Kent to help care for her. Her father, who was still employed, would pay for their food until Caesar could find employment locally. On the day the letter arrived, Caesar had been to the docks looking for work and had been hired as a ships steward. He was ecstatic to be back in the job he loved, and back at sea. He couldn't wait to tell Rebecca. She would be able to leave Mrs Peters service and together they could rent rooms near the docks.

Two days later and Rebecca's day off was spent in the park with Caesar trying to decide what it would be best to do. There was no doubt that Rebecca would be going to Kent, she would never let her parents down when they needed her. Caesar's choice was far harder. If he moved to Kent with his wife and child, employment wasn't guaranteed and his father-in-law's wage wouldn't provide for three extra mouths indefinitely. Taking the job on the ship would mean living apart from his family and travelling to Kent to be with them when the ship docked.

It was August 12th 1847 and as the blue sky gave way to dismal rain clouds she slipped her arm through his as together they walked down to the docks, Rebecca was saying a tearful goodbye to Caesar. She was going to Kent and on the 14th he would be boarding the ship "The Diamond" bound for Barbados. His wage was £2.10s which was to be advanced to him on entry and would be sent to Rebecca.

The crew list for this ship shows that Caesar was listed as Peter. Whether his African accent was difficult to understand or the master was hard of hearing, Caesar never found out. He didn't care what name he went by, he was just grateful that he was employed.

In Kent Rebecca fell into the daily routine of looking after her young daughter and caring for her sick mother who doted on her only grandchild. Her eyes would sparkle every time the child went to her, to have her nose wiped or a shoe fastened. Sometimes it was to give grandmother a posy of wild flowers that Rebecca had helped her pluck from the hedge row whilst walking to the market.

Five months after returning to Eastry, Rebecca's mother had her first heart attack. She had insisted on helping with the weekly wash despite Rebecca's protests and whilst trying to wring the water out of John's "Sunday best" clothes, she had fallen onto the concrete floor of the scullery clutching her chest.

After calling a neighbour to keep an eye on her little daughter, Rebecca ran the length of the High Street and hammered on the doctor's door. She had no idea how they were going to pay for his services all she could think about was getting immediate help for her mother. By nightfall when John had returned from work, his wife was sleeping soundly. The colour in her cheeks had returned to a pale pink instead of the ghastly grey it had been.

Over the next few months as the last days of winter slowly turned to spring and blustery April showers filled the sky, Charlotte seemed to return to full health. On warmer days she would sit on the front doorstep and with her namesake, watching and waving to the villagers making their way to and from Sandwich. Many would stop for a chat and ruffle the dark curls of the little girl's hair. Rebecca was relieved that her mother no longer seemed to need the services of the doctor. Neither she nor her father complained about having to pay for her mothers well–being, they would do anything for her, but money was a problem. The £15 Mr. Langdon had left them was all but gone now.

Since he went into the Merchant Navy Caesar had been able to come home twice, and on both occasions he had given her all the money he could, some of which went on tuition fees for Charlotte. The only money he kept for himself was the rent for a room in London where he stayed when the period between sailings was too short to allow him to make the journey to Eastry. To ensure that there would be at least a little spare cash should her Mother ever need the doctor again, Rebecca knew she would have to find work, which would be difficult with a small child to care for. The only option she had, like many people, was to take in washing. The people from the house opposite were often asking for help and it was there that she found employment.

Christmas week of 1848 found Caesar on his way to join his wife at her parent's home. Tucked into his bag with his uniform was his gift to Rebecca, a copy of *A Christmas Carol* by Charles Dickens which Caesar had bought from one of his shipmates.

For Charlotte he had a small doll dressed in a purple, silk dress complete with a sash, and lace trim. Her hair was worn in ringlets and on her feet she had black shoes with white silk rosettes. The dolls clothes were faded and threadbare in places, but he knew that either Rebecca or her mother could make the whole thing presentable. A clay pipe and thick shawl were for his in-laws.

All the family were up early Christmas morning, thanks to Charlotte who at five years old was very excited: not only was her beloved daddy home but it was Christmas as well. Unable to afford a Christmas tree, Rebecca's father had found a large branch, stripped it of its remaining leaves and stood it in a bucket in the corner of the tiny front parlour. From this hung bows made by Rebecca's mother from pieces of rag, plus six crackers, which were invented by a London sweet maker, Tom Smith in 1846.

They sat down to a Christmas dinner of roast goose bought from the local farm, and potatoes and vegetables from their own garden. They thought themselves quite lucky to have had such a spread. Their neighbours, unable to find well-paying employment were making do with rabbit, which the head of the house had spent a long time snaring. After dinner it was time for church and the whole village turned out for the singing of Christmas carols there. Charlotte's favourite was *Silent Night*. She felt very proud of herself because she knew nearly all of the words and with her head held high sang really loudly.

The decorated tree branch was stripped bare and the wood used on the fire. The rag bows were put away on top of a cupboard and the best china, washed dried and put into the dresser in the scullery.

On Friday the 5th January, Caesar left Eastry in readiness to join the ship "The Jewess". Rebecca, with his beautiful daughter by her side waved until he turned the corner and they could no longer see him.

The slight snowfall of the previous week had melted, much to Charlotte's dismay and Rebecca's relief; she had work enough without mopping the floors every time Charlotte went in and out of the garden. Then, when every one thought the winter had passed, a frightening snowstorm hit the South East in April 1849. Carts and wagons were stuck fast in snowdrifts, men and boys digging desperately to free them while women frantically swept snow from doorsteps and paths. John, unable to go to work helped clear the way from Walton Cottage along the lane to the next village. Other men cleared the road in the opposite direction from Eastry Cross to the village of Northbourne. Returning home late in the afternoon John couldn't help but notice how drawn and tired Rebecca looked, he also heard her being sick every morning and didn't have to ask what the trouble was. As July arrived Rebecca unpacked the parcel under her bed and took from it all the little baby clothes that Charlotte had once worn. Rebecca's second child would be born in a few weeks.

With the baby would come extra laundry and she wondered whether September would be giving plenty of sunshine and beautiful autumnal skies, or rain and gale-force winds. If the weather held she could dry the clothes outside as there was little enough room in the small scullery now with the washing she took in. Several lines of thick string ran from wall to wall at varying heights to accommodate the daily washing which Rebecca started at 4am before making breakfast for her father at 5am. Once he had gone to work she would wake Charlotte, give her breakfast then send her to school after which she would make her mothers breakfast at about 9am, and after washing her hands and face would make her comfortable in the chair by the window. Some days, when her mother was feeling stronger, she would ask Rebecca to help her downstairs where she would sit in the parlour and speak about days gone by.

A daughter, Caroline was born at her grandparent's home in Eastry on September 19th 1849 and was nearly a year old before her father Caeser saw her. He was working harder than ever now and had very few days off before being signed up for another ship. It was August 1850 and Charlotte saw him before he had reached the house and had gone running to meet him, her black curls bobbing up and down, her face lit up by her smile. Caesar lifted his daughter onto his broad shoulders and carried her back to the house wishing that just once his parents could see her. He knew they would adore her. He could imagine his father explaining the customs of Sierra Leone and his mother telling her about the wild animals such as bush pigs, monkeys and porcupines, or explaining about the dangers of the rivers wherein crocodiles and hippopotamuses lurked.

Caesar was glad to be home. He couldn't wait to see their second child and was amazed to see Caroline standing up, holding on to the seat of a chair. Immediately smitten, he bent down to lift her into his arms and was horrified to hear the child scream and hold her arms out to her mother. He realised then that he was just a stranger to his little daughter; it was in September, just before he left Eastry to rejoin his ship that his youngest child started to call him Papa. Rebecca hated the fact that although she was married, her husband was always away but knew that there was no other option,. Like thousands of other wives whose husbands were in the Merchant Navy, it was something she had to cope with.

Chapter 13

When her father had gone to work one Saturday in November 1850, Charlotte was playing in the scullery and the baby was still sleeping, so Rebecca decided to take her mother's breakfast up to her. She knew as soon as she opened the door to her parent's bedroom. Her mother was lying on her side looking at her with unseeing eyes, in her hand a picture of John. Rebecca went to the bed and gently closed her mother's eyelids, kissed her still-warm lips, drew the cover over her head and with tears streaming down her face went downstairs.

Charlotte's funeral, a simple affair, took place at Eastry Church on 9th November 1850 followed by a gathering of a few of her friends at Walton Cottage.

John Mills sat quietly in the corner of the parlour trying to come to terms with the fact that he would never see his beloved wife again. He had been married to Charlotte for 38 years and just couldn't imagine life without her, and would forever long to hear her laughter and her soft singing as she went about her daily chores. "Time heals", he was told by a well meaning neighbour, but not as quickly as the soft hands of children reaching out to touch the cheeks of a grandfather who looks so sad. John's granddaughters did this and he realised then that life would go on, but in a very different way. After putting on their warmest outdoor clothes he let his eldest granddaughter lead him to the front door while Caroline toddled unsteadily behind. Once outside he lifted the baby into his arms and, still clutching the older child's hand as if for comfort, walked the short distance to the park.

John Mills watched with pride as both of his granddaughters grew into thoughtful, polite children. Charlotte in particular was a stunning looking child having inherited her mother's graceful ways, slim, tiny build and Caesar's full lips and tight curls. The younger child was every bit as pretty but was prone to sulking and forever asking why she couldn't be the same colour as the other children. They would sit and never tire of hearing the story of how he and Grandmother Charlotte had met or about the awful life that she had when slavers had captured her. He told the girls of the Tuareg people and their customs, asked that they never forget their roots and be very proud of who they were and where they came from.

He knew that some local people, children and adults, had made remarks about the girls colour and hoped that they would be able to cope with this. John had always felt that as Caesar was away most of the time it was he who should, and would, protect the girls and be their father figure. Sadly, this was a role that he played only for a short while.

Two years and five months after the death of his beloved Charlotte, John Mills died of heart disease. On the evening of 16th April 1853 after leaving his gardening job at the end of a busy week John walked across the road to his house, took his boots off and left them at the door. He was sitting in the parlour waiting for his daughter to bring his customary mug of tea before his evening meal. Rebecca was in the scullery when she heard him call her name followed by a low groan of pain. She immediately went to him and made him as comfortable as she could before calling to Charlotte to look after her sister. At the doctor's house Rebecca explained what had happened and together they returned to Walton Cottage.

John was seventy-five years old. He was buried on 23rd April 1853. In less than three years a distraught Rebecca had buried both parents.

They were together again, this time forever.

Chapter 14

Caesar had been back in Kent for three and a half months, the longest he had been at home with his family and was saddened at how much of his children's lives he had missed. Back in his native Sierra Leone, fathers were the ones who taught their children the ways of life and he couldn't help but think that he should have been doing just that. For him, it was a choice of being a servant or a ship's steward and the latter paid better wages, which meant that he could provide adequately for his family.

Rebecca was three months pregnant when he returned to London to board the ship "The British Isles" which sailed to Demerara in the West Indies. He hoped that he would be back in England for the birth of his third child and he was. Caesar had journeyed back to his home on 29th June 1854 and Rebecca gave birth to their son the next day. James John was as handsome as his sisters were beautiful with the same big brown eyes and skin that looked and felt like brown velvet. The girls were now 11 and five years old and desperately wanted to hold the baby so, telling them both to sit on the bed, Caesar proudly but gently laid James John in their laps.

The following three days were spent tidying the garden, a large area covering seven perches. Rebecca had kept the garden immaculate with a small flower border just outside the door and rows of potatoes, cabbages and carrots further down the garden but Caesar knew it would be a while before his wife would be able to tend the garden and the owner of the cottage liked his properties to be well maintained.

When his son was only four days old, Caesar returned once again to London to join his ship, which once more was heading for Demerara. The two girls were allowed to go to the end of the road with him now they were older, provided they went straight back home afterwards. With one daughter sitting on his shoulders and the other clasping his large hand, they set off. Half an hour later the girls were back home.

Life for Rebecca went on in its usual way. Charlotte was a great help to her now, looking after her siblings as well as doing some of the household chores. When the weather was nice she took her brother out to toddle round the garden, carefully holding his hand. It wasn't long before James John took his first steps unaided and soon he was following Charlotte everywhere. Charlotte was absolutely besotted with her brother and never tired of being with him. He in turn would smile a smile that lit his whole face whenever he saw his sister. The bond between them would last a lifetime.

With every passing year the village increased in size as more people came to Kent looking for work on the farms that were scattered in and around the area. Eastry chalk mine, a lime burning business also brought fresh faces to the village.

As the village grew, so too did the comments about race and colour. James John was too young to understand the comments but Rebecca could see the hurt on her daughters faces. She explained that the people who were rude to them had not been taught that all people are equal.

"Never stoop as low," she told her children, *"as to retaliate by name-calling. We are clean both in mind and body as are our clothes. We didn't choose the colour of our skin, the good*

Lord chose that so be proud and hold your head up high."

Caesar returned home at the end of January 1857 and stayed until the beginning of March. On the eve of his departure Rebecca had baked bread and pastries for him, enough to last until he was back on board ship again. Lying in bed that night after showing their love for each other, he cuddled up behind her and kissed the nape of her neck as they both fell asleep.

The all too familiar morning sickness started at the end of May and Rebecca knew that a fourth addition to their family was growing inside her.

Harriett Ann Rebecca was born on the bitterly cold evening of November 8th 1857. The other three children were awoken by the hearty cries of their newborn sister at 10.30pm. Charlotte, after pressing her finger to her lips to warn Caroline and James John to keep very quiet crept across to her mother's bedroom to see what was happening. She was just in time to see their neighbour Mrs Court clearing old papers and rags from the bed and her mother putting the baby to her breast. The same dark eyes and skin and the same mop of black curly hair, Harriett was another beautiful Fitzgerald child. Her baptism took place at Eastry Church on 6th December 1857. She wore the same little gown that the other three children had worn at their baptisms - a traditional gown made of ivory coloured silk with a pretty lace trimmed bodice on the front and back and a matching silk bonnet. The other three children and their parents all had their Sunday clothes on and with Charlotte holding her little brother's hand they made their way to the pews nearest the font.

Charlotte started work at the Union Workhouse when she was just 14 years old. She spent her days having orders barked at her by all and sundry, but realised she was far luckier than the unfortunate people who were unlucky enough to find themselves actually living in this formidable place.

Workhouses were usually based on Sir Francis Head's courtyard plan and designed to accommodate 500 inmates including the elderly, infirm and children. Charlotte worked hard, never complained about her red raw hands and aching back. Being such a tiny slender girl, the work (especially when she was assigned to the laundry room) was extremely heavy. Her working day started at 6.30am and ended at 7pm. She worked six days a week and happily gave her mother more than half of her wage. Although the work was hard, not seeing her beloved young brother was even harder. He was in bed when she left for and returned from work and she missed him a lot. On her day off she would help her mother with the family chores and with these finished her time was spent reading to her little brother from their favourite book, entitled *Snowflakes and Sunbeams*. James John was still only three years old and didn't understand any of it, but as Charlotte turned the pages he would clap his chubby hands together and smile up at his sister.

The seasons came and went, each bringing its own delights. Beneath bare trees in autumn lay thick carpets of red, yellow and brown leaves, in winter the brilliant red berries of the holly bushes, while shyly hanging their heads towards the ground were the delicate white snowdrops. Soon daffodils and crocuses broke through the cool earth competing for the first glimpse of the spring sun, followed a few months later by the scent of summer roses. Christmases and birthdays rolling one year into another until three years had past.

Caesar returned home whenever he could and was always amazed at how his children had changed in looks and personality. Charlotte was quite the young lady now, taking on an air of importance since finding employment and contributing to the household bills. The lads in the village had started showing an interest in her and before long she would be stepping out with one of them. Her parents hoped that she would choose wisely.

Caroline was 11, still sulky and prone to stamping her feet when she was told she couldn't do something she wanted to. Even at her young age, she had an air of superiority about her and thought it quite awful that her sister should be doing such a menial job. She had informed everyone that she would do far better herself.

The broad smile, dancing eyes and spirited nature told Caesar that his six year old son was always going to find some sort of mischief to get into. He had started school and appeared to be doing well. Perhaps his high spirits would diminish, as he grew older but even if they didn't, Caesar would always be proud of his only boy and James John loved to be at his father's side when Caesar was home from the sea.

His youngest, 3 year old Harriett was so close to her mother that she cried every time Caesar went near her. She didn't know him and certainly wanted nothing to do with him.

The first week of 1861 saw the initial signs that Caroline was desperately unhappy, she hated living in the village and going to the local school. It was easy for her mother as an adult to tell her to take no notice or ignore others when the jibes about her skin colour started. To a child, however, trying to fit in and make friends it was a totally different matter.

One of Rebecca's relatives, Mary, had married William Nethersole, a publican, and lived at the Hare and Hounds public house at Northbourne. Once or twice a month Rebecca and the children would walk the country lanes from Eastry to visit and catch up on any family news. A middle aged couple they looked forward to Rebecca's visits as they enjoyed her company and loved the children. This childless couple welcomed Caroline into their lives and home with open arms, they admired this bright 12 year old girl who knew what she wanted out of life. They would ensure that she had a good education and an excellent upbringing.

Over the next three years, nothing changed a great deal within the Fitzgerald household. Rebecca was still working, as was Charlotte. James John was a pupil at Eastry School, Caroline was still living at Northbourne and being educated privately.

Harriett was also at school. A slow clumsy child, she had difficulty with some of the lessons - she loved arithmetic but didn't like reading. What she dreaded most was spelling lessons. No matter how hard she tried, she just couldn't get her spellings right.

Chapter 15

It was July 1864. A messenger from the shipping company bought Rebecca the news that every seafarers wife feared, Caesar had died and been buried at sea. At that moment in time Rebecca felt the world had stopped. She stood on the doorstep of their little home watching the movement of the messenger's lips, yet hearing nothing. Her eyes became fixated on a tiny insect that was being washed down the messenger's cheek in a droplet of sweat. In her head the words died at sea, played over and over again.

A few months later Rebecca received Caesar's final wages, which upon his death had been forwarded to the Board of Trade. His personal belongings were destroyed on the day he died. No more would he come through the door of their little home, his bag flung over one shoulder. No more stories for her and their children about his travels to faraway lands. No churchyard grave as a final resting place. Nowhere she could go and place flowers. Not even the chance to say goodbye.

The months and years passed in a blur of trying to keep up the payments on the house and keeping the two younger children fed and clothed. Charlotte was still employed and was now giving her mother most of her wages each week. Every spring they tended the garden together, planting vegetables that were then picked and stored for use over the coming months. Clothes that were once considered past repair were given a new lease of life by shortening a sleeve or lengthening a bodice, socks were darned over darns. The two younger children hated all of this. It drew more attention to their looks and consequently affected not only their home life but also their schooling.

Caroline was affected the least by her father's death. She was doing extremely well at school and had already been found a place to learn fine embroidery and needlework. Thriving in the over abundance of love and gifts showered on her by the Nethersole family she knew her clothes would never be patched. When they wore out, they were simply replaced. She missed her father, but didn't dwell on his death. She had a life to live and she swore it would not be the sort of life her mother had.

Although academically as bright as his older sister, James John was far more trouble. Unable to come to terms with the loss of his father, he had started on a downward spiral almost immediately. All he thought about was leaving school. His once immaculate schoolwork gradually became a mess or wasn't completed at all. Charlotte tried speaking to her brother,

"Everyone is concerned about where all this is going to end, James. All the family are hurting over the loss of our father but at times like these, we should try and do our best so that he would still be proud of us."

"I know what I do is wrong," replied James John, "I will try harder, I promise"

For a while things changed as the boy tried to mend his ways. It wasn't always easy as apart from Harriett, he was the only other child of a different colour in the school. He instinctively knew that at times he was singled out for ridicule from his peers. When he retaliated, he was punished. It became a never ending circle.

On 16th January 1866 the Headmaster wrote in the Boys School Log Book,

"Obliged to punish Fitzgerald before the whole school for lying and determined disobedience. I hope that the good whipping he has received brings this willful boy to his senses quicker and better than anything else and possibly he may never need it again."

An entry for the 22nd February reads,

"I have noticed today that Fitzgerald has been more diligent and attentive."

James John's good behaviour didn't last long and in April he received yet more punishment, again for lying.

Rebecca was summoned to school two months later on Friday 15th June.

"James John," said the master shaking his head, *"is becoming a bad influence on the other children and should he continue with this type of conduct, the punishment will be more severe than just a whipping."*

James John came home from school that day to find his mother with red rimmed eyes. He knew he was the cause of her sorrow.

"I promise I really will change my ways Mother," he vowed.

"James John, you have to," replied Rebecca, *"I am paying 2d every Monday for your schooling, which I can ill afford, but am spending because I want you to be able to find decent employment when the time comes."*

The following months saw a marked improvement in the boy. A family named Love had moved into the village and their son and James John became great friends. The Love family accepted that their son's new friend was dark skinned because they didn't see that as a problem. The two boys went everywhere together and were always at each other's houses helping in the gardens, chopping logs or just sitting on the back door step idly chatting. Rebecca thought the troubles with her headstrong son were a thing of the past. This changed in May 1867 when Rebecca was called to the school where she and Mrs Love were told that both boys had been absent for most of the previous week and were still not at school. Rebecca was devastated.

In July of that year, James John's dream of leaving school was half way to becoming reality. He had found employment as a postman and as such would only be attending school in the mornings. The following week as James John handed his wage to Rebecca she thought of how useful the extra money would be and hoped that part-time schooling would make a difference to her son's attitude. For a few weeks his schoolwork improved but in September, Rebecca once more found herself in the head teacher's office. Standing behind the huge oak desk she heard James John called, troublesome, lazy and extremely insolent, and for several days she could hardly bring herself to speak to her son. She felt he had let her down terribly. Over and over she thought of how things might have been, had Caesar lived.

From the beginning of March 1868 James John and several others in his class were at work far more than they were at school, for some they were now the main wage-earners, for others their wage topped up the money that the particular household had coming in. Poverty caused attendance problems for many in the school .Some children had to look after their younger siblings while the mothers went to work. Others arrived at school exhausted after getting up to work at 3 or 4am working on the farms till 8.30am.

On his last day at school in the School Log Book, James John, determined not to conform to any rules, had the following written after his name:

Class 1: *James John Fitzgerald has been very incorrect.*

In time Harriett was "presented for examination" at school and how she hated it. Everyday school work was bad enough but this was even worse. She couldn't even answer questions that she knew the answers to. Her mouth suddenly went dry, a nerve in her leg started twitching and to make matters even worse she could feel the gritty like substance under her eyelids that told her she was going to cry.

One year later and things were not getting any better, in July 1867; she was reprimanded having *"spelt 13 words wrongly"*. Harriett, like her brother, couldn't wait to leave school. By 1869 she had achieved a Standard III in her education but wasn't sure whether Standard III was average or not, if it was below average there was not much she could do about it.

"Harriett," pleaded her mother, "think about what I have told you about the importance of a good education, without that education you will only ever be offered jobs that the more educated turn down or won't even apply for."

Harriett shrugged her shoulders. When she finally left school the only work she could find was that of a laundress.

Chapter 16

The year was 1868. Charlotte said to her mother "I really don't want anything to eat before going to work, I don't feel well."

"You didn't eat anything yesterday morning either did you?" replied Rebecca, "What's wrong with you?"

Her daughter didn't answer.

That evening, mother and daughter were in the scullery after finishing the last of the chores, when suddenly, Rebecca closed the door.

Looking her daughter straight in the eyes she asked, "When is the baby due, who is the father?"

Charlotte put her head down and began to sob.

"It's too late to cry now, young lady!" shouted her mother, "You should never have got yourself into this situation in the first place."

"Who are you to judge?" sobbed Charlotte, "Weren't you unmarried when you became pregnant with me?"

Rebecca felt herself softening towards her daughter and putting her hands gently on her shoulders said, "I should not have shouted at you, shouting will not make anything better, but I really hoped that you would be spared them shame of being unmarried and pregnant. Have you decided what you are going to do now?"

"The baby's father, who delivers supplies to the workhouse, has been courting me for five months," Charlotte explained, "He told me that he loved me and I gave myself to him quite willingly. I didn't expect the act of love making to have been so rough or uncaring. Nor did I want to make love in the back of a cart down dark lanes, but he told me that if I really did love him, I would lay down with him anywhere. I did love him and so whenever or wherever the opportunity arose I made love with him. When I told him that I thought I was pregnant he was furious and said the child wasn't his and he has refused to even look at me since. I don't know what I am going to do."

Charlotte bust into tears as her mother took her in her arms and stroked her thick black hair. She told her daughter that everything would be fine, that between them they would bring this child up even though it would be an awful struggle.

A son was born to Charlotte on 16th May 1869. She named him Arthur Holder Fitzgerald; she gave him the second name Holder so that people would know the surname of the baby's absent father. Four days later Charlotte was back at work, her mother having care of the baby during the day. She soon learnt though, that when an illegitimate child was born it was always the mother that was the dirty one, the loose one, never the father, the father could walk away. The endless stares, sniggering and whispering began immediately followed by comments or obscenities.

"Where's your half-caste bastard son?" shouted some of the villagers.

Other people whispered in loud voices, so Charlotte could not help but hear, "Look at her, she's nothing but a whore, she's not fit to mix with the decent people of the village."

Charlotte could no longer cope with the taunts and decided she would leave the area. Her employer was sorry to see her leave, she was a trustworthy, reliable worker and had been with them for several years. After failing to persuade her to stay, he told her of an establishment where she might find employment as a cleaner in a large house that an acquaintance of his owned if she could find someone to care for her baby.

After a tearful goodbye to her son, a thank you kiss to her mother in whose care she left him and a long hug for her brother, Charlotte set off for Hawkhurst. With two stops, both at Inns to allow passengers and horses to rest it was a long and uneventful journey. Her new job was much like her old one. Her master was a big man with a red bulbous nose and a squint in one eye. He was not very friendly and tended to grunt rather than speak but paid a fair wage and that was what was important to Charlotte. She had to send money home, her mother could not afford to keep Arthur for nothing and nor would Charlotte expect her to.

The routine at her new place of employment would have been quite mundane but for the presence of the groom. A black haired, dark skinned lad with smouldering grey eyes, James Mitten never smiled but whenever he saw Charlotte; he would look her up and down giving her a quick wink. Charlotte for her part looked forward to seeing him when he came into the kitchen for his meals.

Soon it was the Christmas period and Boxing Day found Charlotte back in Kent with her family. She was amazed at how much her son had grown and how close he was to her own mother. She felt such heaviness in her heart as she thought of the time she had been away from him and knew that it was time that could never be recaptured. She had missed his first tooth breaking his baby gums, his first attempt at sitting and crawling and she knew she wouldn't be there when he took his first step either. The day went far too quickly and soon it was late afternoon, time to return to Hawkhurst. Charlotte sat in the tiny parlour with her infant son on her lap. Burying her face in his dark silky curls she breathed in his sweet baby smell and wished she didn't have to leave him.

James Mitten was 19 and she was five years older. He asked her about her life and her family, most of what he wanted to know, Charlotte told him. She didn't tell him about Arthur, there was time for that later, after all they had only just started walking out together. It was in January when they first made love, she should have told him then about her baby, but she didn't. By April she knew she would have to tell him that she carrying his baby and she also had a child at home.

James was livid that she hadn't told him about Arthur. He then gave her a choice, marry him but leave Arthur with her mother or they could both go their separate ways. He had no intention of raising another man's child. He would give her a week to think things over. It was him or the child. For Charlotte, there was no option. She could never go through the humiliation of giving birth to yet another bastard child.

Rebecca was furious with her daughter, she could not believe that she was pregnant again and about to abandon her first born child.

"Mother, I promise that we will try to send a little money to help clothe and feed Arthur," Charlotte promised.

"Your child," spat Rebecca, "is not my responsibility, but now you have made him just that. How am I supposed to care for him? What am I going to tell him when he asks about his parents and why they didn't want him?"

Angry words were shouted from daughter to mother and back again. Words that should never have been spoken, the row that followed lasted for several years.

Charlotte and James were married in Eastry Church, a still angry Rebecca refused to attend. John James and Caroline acted as witnesses to the couple and although both of them could see the predicament Charlotte had managed to find herself in, they too wondered how she could abandon her little son. This was a tiny person that she had given birth to and she should, by the very laws of nature be there to cherish him and watch him grow.

The newly married couple returned to Hawkhurst where James was now employed as a farm labourer. The hours were long and arduous, the wage very poor. Unable to find accommodation they lived with James's parents, not an ideal situation as James brothers and sisters still lived at home, making living conditions so cramped that a younger brother slept in the same room as the newlyweds.

With the arrival of their baby, Lily Mary Mitten in 1870 the house was so crowded that there was no room for her crib, instead the baby slept in her parent's bed. By 1872 they had a house of their own where Charlotte gave birth to another son Herbert James. Two years later William John was born. The family attended the parish church at the south end of the village, the older part of Hawkhurst and it was there that their children were baptised.

Shortly after the birth of his second son James Mitten lost his job at the farm. The invention of the threshing machine to help farming had reduced the need for farm workers and many men were forced out of work. James moved his family and soon found employment as a groom looking after the horses that helped bring the oysters ashore in Whitstable, a fishing port, on the North Kent coast of England. At Island Wall, Whitstable in a small, wood-framed, weatherboard cottage, yards from beach two more sons; Edward Joseph and James Henry were born. With the birth of each child the money sent to Rebecca for the care of Arthur became less and less until finally it stopped altogether.

Chapter 17

A sad lonely eight year old child Arthur would sit and speak to anyone who would pass the time of day with him. He had been told about his mother from an early age and now that was all he wanted; his mum. Arthur hadn't seen his mother for over two years now, but he could still remember her. His daydreams were always about the time he would be able to live with her. He knew he wasn't really wanted at his grandmothers, not that his grandmother didn't love him, she just didn't have time to take notice of him.

Rebecca was getting too old and far too worn down with the strain of trying to keep Harriett, Arthur and herself fed and clothed. At times she would look at her grandson with a mixture of hatred and resentment. She thought that if he were not living with them she could take life a little easier, not have to work quite so hard. Now over 60 years old she felt she had earned a rest. At other times when he smiled his shy lopsided smile showing perfectly placed pearl white teeth she would run her gnarled hands through his thick black unruly ringlets, while crying inside for all the things that were wrong in her grandson's life. Rebecca would then resolve to take more notice of Arthur and try and be more loving towards him, make sure his clothes were clean and mended and he was up and ready for school. Unfortunately these resolutions never lasted more that a day or two before the resentment started building up in Rebecca again. She wrote to her daughter in Whitstable telling Charlotte that she could not cope any longer and as his mother, Arthur should be living with her.

The following week, his few belongings having been packed, Arthur was put on the cart for the journey to his mothers. The young lad was very pleased to be going. To be part of the ever growing family in Whitstable was all Arthur wanted. He waited impatiently by the side of the lane for the cart to arrive, hopping from one foot to the other while wiping his runny nose on his sleeve and praying he wouldn't wet his breeches through excitement. At the sound of the horse's hooves clipping along the road Arthur called to his grandmother who came to give him a quick kiss on the forehead, after which the boy climbed up into the cart and without a backward glance, settled down on one of the rough wooden seats.

Charlotte awaited her eldest son's arrival with some trepidation. She wasn't sure whether she was looking forward to having him live with them or not. Such a long time had passed and although he was her flesh and blood, the bonding between mother and child had never really taken place. The other children had seen him on a few occasions and they all seemed to get on together, but would it still be the same if Arthur was living with them permanently? Then of course there was her husband James, he had not wanted the child to live with them at all. The boy was after all just another mouth for him to feed and more work for Charlotte. After giving Arthur a curt nod on his arrival, James wasted no time in telling him that he was none too pleased to see him and if he didn't behave he would send him to the Workhouse. Arthur wasn't sure what the Workhouse was, but he didn't like the sound of it and promised he would be good.

After a month things had settled down in the Mitten household. Arthur made sure he kept out of James's way. He attended school regularly, spoke only when spoken to, and helped in the house and around the garden. James gradually softened towards the lad and six months later let him accompany him to the stables where man and boy would sit together for a while. James took great pride caring for the horses and would spend hours carefully grooming them. Arthur watched his stepfather intently and was told that when he was older and had learnt how, he could try his hand at grooming them as well. With the work finished James and Arthur would walk to the beach and the public house called The Old Neptune. James would buy ale for himself and allow the lad to have a mouthful, laughing as the boy pulled a face when the strong ale hit his taste buds. With this ritual over, they would make their way back home. At other times when James was not at work he would take Arthur and his own boys and sit and watch the trains, something which the boys loved doing. The railway had been conceived as an alternative means to the turnpike road for the carrying of coal and merchandise between Canterbury and Whitstable. George Stephenson's son, Robert Stephenson had supervised the construction work that took some four years to complete before it was formally opened in the 1830s.

Arthur was happier than he had been in all his short life. He adored his younger brothers and although his half-sister, Lily Mary was forever bossing him about he didn't mind, some days they fought and didn't like each other at all, other days they were partners in crime. Against all odds the Mitten household was a happy one.

In May of 1879 their mother told them that they were soon to have a new baby brother or sister. Lily Mary stated that it had better be a girl, she had enough brothers already.

As the months went on, it was apparent that there was something very wrong with Charlotte. She was so thin no-one believed her when she said she was pregnant. Ashen faced and always tired, she looked old beyond her years. The chores she had done with such ease in the past she could only half finish now. On many occasions dinner wasn't on the table when James returned from work. Washing wasn't done and the children were left to cope as best they could. Lily Mary would spend her free time caring for the younger boys whilst Arthur would sweep, tidy and clean the hearths. Two months before her baby was due Dr Williams diagnosed Charlotte as having an inflammation of the membrane of the middle ear. The whole family felt better for knowing this. At last, with the help of some medicine Charlotte would soon be on the road to recovery. Or so they thought. Charlotte got worse and in August, she was diagnosed as having chronic peritonitis.

A tiny girl with the same black curly hair and dark eyes as her mother was born to Charlotte and James on the 15th of September 1879 in Whitstable. There was no doctor in attendance but a friend of the family, Mary Foad, had come to help with the birth. The older children, on returning from school, were told to take James Henry the youngest child into the garden and stay there until they were told they could come in. Upstairs they could hear the cries of the newborn baby and were longing to see her.

Moments later Mary shouted, "Lily Mary run to your father's place of work and tell him to return home as quickly as he can! Arthur, you are to make haste to Dr Bruce's home and ask that he come and attend to your Mother immediately. Go on, quickly now."

Picking up the baby, Mary washed her before laying her into the wicker baby carriage that had been placed next to the bed and covered her with the shawl that Charlotte had spend many nights making for this latest addition. Putting her fist to her mouth the newborn child sucked noisily and immediately fell asleep.

Turning to the bed that was covered with the bloody mess that accompanies a difficult birth, Mary took the hand of the figure that was lying there. Desperately she searched for a pulse and having found nothing she took the looking glass from the chest of draws and held it in front of Charlotte mouth. There was no sign of the cloudiness that breath makes on a cold surface, no rise and fall of her chest. Mary knew that Charlotte was dead and after pushing the still damp curls away from her cheeks she pulled the blanket gently over her friends beautiful face. Picking up the sleeping baby she went down the narrow staircase, called the other children in and sat with them awaiting the arrival of Dr Bruce.

With the funeral over and the last of the neighbours having returned to their own homes, James was at last left alone with his and Charlotte's relatives. The talk was of what he was going to do with seven children. He had to work to keep a roof over his head. None of the family lived near so could not help with the day to day running of the house which included looking after the children. Neighbours offered to look after some of the children for James but he knew that they had children of their own and would soon tire of his. There was only one option apart from the workhouse.

His married sister would take James Henry. Only two years old he was young enough to adapt to life without his natural parents. James's brother offered to raise Edward with his own three boys.

Lily Mary, Herbert and William would stay with their father. A young widower who lived close by would, for a small payment look after the children during the day, returning them to their father in the evenings.

James John Fitzgerald (Unknown photographer)

Having discussed everything with each other and other concerned family members, James John Fitzgerald and his wife Annie who had been married for a little over a year, eagerly agreed to take the newborn baby and raise her as their own.

After attending the funeral and crying for a sister who had thought so much of him, James John watched his wife gently lift his tiny niece out of her carriage. Annie wrapped blankets round the child and carefully holding the back of her head for support, lifted her up for James Mitten to give his baby daughter a goodbye kiss. By the time they arrived back at their home in Eythorne, Kent they had named her Elizabeth Anne and loved her as if she were their very own.

The only problem now for James Mitten, was Arthur.

An Illegitimate child, Arthur was parentless now his mother was dead. Although James had grown quite fond of the boy, he wasn't his son and so wasn't his responsibility. Rebecca was his next of kin and as such she was asked to give him a home.

Chapter 18

When the day came for him to return to Eastry, Arthur cried and pleaded with James to let him stay with him. "Haven't I been very good?" the boy asked. "I promise I wont be any trouble at all, please let me stay here, please."

James, as he strode towards the open door on his way to work replied, "Sorry lad, it's just not possible, you belong with your own family."

Arthur never saw the man that he had grown to love as a father again.

The young boy became sullen and disobedient after returning to his grandmother's house. Rebecca screamed at him. Shouted, pleaded and bribed him. Sometimes she would resort to thrashing him. He didn't cry, just stood there with a look of sadness on his face. He knew his grandmother couldn't cope and didn't really want him. Lying in bed at night he would think of the happy times he had with his brothers and sister. Remembering the days he had spent watching his step-father groom the horses. Dream of what might have been if only his mother hadn't died. He hated his life now, the hell of going to school where every day he was called a "darkie bastard" by some of the older children. He didn't really know what the words meant but they sounded nasty to him. All he knew was the other children wouldn't let him join in any games, shouting at him, "Clear off, you haven't got a father and we aren't allowed to play with you."

Many of the adults in the village ignored him believing he would pollute other children because he had been born in disgrace and wasn't the same colour as them so therefore must be bad.

Rebecca had grown quite accustomed to the school complaining about the amount of education Arthur was missing. She knew that after a caning, he would attend school for a day or two before going back to his old ways. It was as if history was repeating its self - the school was the same, just a different child.

As the weeks went by Arthur was spending more and more time away from home. Sometimes he would wander aimlessly through the village. Often he would be marched to school after being found hiding by one of the local people. Most days though he would walk into Sandwich, if he was careful he could spend all day there and no one would see him. Wandering along the Ropewalk, onward to the Guildhall and then into the market place, his last stopping place was always St. Peter's Church. This was his favourite area and he would make his way there in the late afternoon. Sitting amongst the tombstones he would watch the adults going about their chores in the town while children played with hoops or spinning tops.

When the ringing of the church bell sounded at 8pm Arthur would start the long, lonely walk back to Eastry. On fine evenings the slow walk home was pleasant, but as always with the British weather, some evenings were awful. When the storm clouds darkened the skies and angry lightning briefly lit it again, Arthur would wish he had set off for home just a little bit earlier. He knew the lightening would be followed by rolling peals of thunder. Then the rain would fall, drenching him and battering the earth and foliage with a never ending downpour.

Every evening, he knew he would be in for a thrashing from his grandmother. Every morning he knew he would be spending the day in Sandwich again.

Someone else entered Arthur young life a few weeks later, in the form of a young woman called Meg, a pretty, voluptuous prostitute with an abundance of striking red curls. She had been walking near the Fishergate in Sandwich having "done business" with one of the men from the boats there. He was as ugly as sin with the few teeth he possessed hanging like rotting stumps from his gums. His beard had more food in it than she had seen in nearly a week and when he had wrapped his arms around her the smell of his armpits made her want to retch. Still he had offered three coppers so, closing her eyes and thinking of a better life that was yet to come she had earned the coppers. Having received the money she decided she would treat herself to a decent meal, something she hadn't had for the past two days.

She made her way along the road to the Weavers, a building that 16th Century Dutch refugees had used as their home and place of work. She would be eating just beyond there, in a cheap but clean, friendly establishment.

The child was sat on the edge of a grass bank, hugging his knees to his chest. He looked up at her with his large brown sad eyes.

Meg stopped, bent down and put one hand on the child's shoulder, "What's your name?" she asked. "What are you doing here little one, is something wrong?"

That one gesture of kindness was enough to start the child's bottom lip quivering. Try as he might Arthur just not could stop the tears falling, big salty tears that plopped onto his dirt encrusted leg. Meg took the boy by the hand and pulled him to his feet, wrapped her arms around him and held his sobbing body. After a while she took her only kerchief from the pocket inside her cloak, handing it to the child for him to dry his eyes.

With his hands clenched tight at his sides in an attempt

to stop the tears from falling again, he told her what had happened. "My name is Arthur, my Mum died a little while ago and my stepfather said that I couldn't live in their house anymore 'cos I'm not his son. I really miss my half-sister and brothers though; I just want live with them again."

"Where are you living now? Do you attend school?" asked Meg.

"I live with my Grandmother," he replied, "but she's old now and I know she doesn't want me there and I don't want to be there either. I just want my sister and brothers. I don't like going to school, everyone there makes fun of me."

"Well Arthur," she said, gently, "I'm sure your grandmother loves you and even if she is old, I'm sure she is doing the best she can for you. You really have no choice but to stay with her if your stepfather doesn't want you living with him. Now promise me that you will go to school each day and be good for your grandmother. Will you do that?"

Arthur just nodded his head.

"Good lad," smiled Meg, "if you do as I ask you, I will meet you here every Saturday, I'll bring something to eat, then after we have had a walk down by the river, we can have a little picnic. Would you like that?"

"Oh yes, I really would," grinned Arthur.

Half an hour later they had finished the chunk of bread, washed down with a mug of tea that Meg had bought and shared between them. This was all Meg could do for Arthur. It was getting late and she still had "business" to attend to. Smoothing the folds of her stained and threadbare cloak with its moth-eaten fur trim, Meg told the boy to get back to his home.

Meg's attempt at bribing Arthur were fruitless, every day the boy would wait for her, everyday she would scold him for not being at school. Arthur would always promise to go the following day. He never did, so together they would walk through the tiny streets of Sandwich, having something to eat before saying goodbye and going their separate ways. They had known each other for six weeks when the local law officer stopped them, "Meg", he said, hands on his hips, "you do you know you are committing an offence by being on the local highway with a minor, you being a lady of ill-repute and all." She grinned as he went on, "But, I will let you off this time."

"Of course you will, seeing as how you are one of my regulars!" she retorted.

"The lad, though, he's got to come with me," said the officer.

Arthur was grabbed by the scruff of the neck and marched to the Guildhall where he was held whilst the authorities informed his grandmother of his whereabouts.

Two days later on 6th November as she sat in the Wingham Petty Sessions held at the Red Lion Inn waiting to hear her grandson's fate, Rebecca agreed with the authorities she knew she had failed to control and look after the boy. Her statement read:

"I am the grandmother of Arthur Holder Fitzgerald. He is an orphan and lives with me at Eastry. I have to work to keep a roof over the heads of Arthur, my daughter and myself. He is too much to attend to - he is always full of mischief. He will not be controlled, he will not listen and I cannot do anything with him".

Other witnesses gave evidence of thieving and loitering. Arthur protested saying that he only thieved because he was hungry. He was told, in no uncertain terms by the detaining officer that if he was that hungry he should have gone home. When the proceedings finished, Arthur was sentenced to three years in a Reformatory. Rebecca looked towards her grandson, mouthing, "I am so sorry, I do love you."

Arthur looked straight past her to the young woman with

her stained and threadbare cloak, with its moth-eaten fur trim. It was to her that he gave a little smile whilst tears ran down his cheeks as he was led away. It was nearly two months to the day since the death of his mother.

Industrial Schools provided for the education and care of children who were in danger of becoming criminals, disorderly, destitute or vagrants. The Court decided that Arthur was to be sent to Kingsnorth Industrial School, Ashford, Kent which was built in 1875 at a cost of £10,000 and was able to accommodate 200 boys. The Head Schoolmaster was Harry Fairbanks, a formidable man of great height who could stop a boy in his tracks with just one look. A Drill Master and Band Master completed the main staff.

As Arthur's next of kin Rebecca was given the details that related to his admission.

NAME: Arthur Holder Fitzgerald.
AGE: 10 ½ years.
DATE OF ADMISSION: November 6th 1879.
WHERE: Wingham
BY WHOM DETAINED: George J Murray. — S.Musgrave Hilton.
WITH WHAT CHARGED: Refractory.
UNDER WHAT SECTION: 16.
SENTENCE OF DETENTION: 3 Years.
PREVIOUS CHARACTER: ―――――――.
STATE IF ILLEGITIMATE: Yes.

NAMES OF PARENTS OR STEP-PARENTS:

FATHER: Albert Holder.
Mother: Charlotte Eliza Fitzgerald – Dead.
GRANDMOTHER: Rebecca Fitzgerald. Laundress of Eastry,
RELIGIOUS PERSUASION: Protestant.

Rebecca was then taken aside by Mr. Murray, Justice of the Peace and told how serious an offence Arthur had committed and how he was "unruly, unmanageable and resistant to ordinary punishment or stimulus". All of which she had explained in her statement. More than anyone else she knew what Arthur was like, what problems he had. Hadn't she tried her best, unaided to care for the child? How dare this man lecture her! She felt like shouting at him to be quiet.

She left the court in Wingham trying to think of the good that being at Kingsnorth might do her wayward grandson, but none came. His short life had been so troubled and Rebecca knew that those troubles had affected him deeply and wished for his sake that things could have been different.

Chapter 19

The years went by and with each one a new beginning for so many people.

James Mitten married for a second time in 1881, his bride Emma Kelsey, 16 years his senior. With her came her three children, a loveless marriage but one of convenience for both Emma and James. Lily Mary disliked her stepmother with a passion that was difficult to hide. A domineering and harsh woman who ruled the house and punished any child who disobeyed her with the beech switch that stood by the side of the grate. Emma detested Lily Mary to a point of near hatred, she thought she was far too full of herself. She, Emma was the woman of the house now; no slip of a girl was going to get the better of her. Lily Mary could not settle and longed for the times when James and Annie would bring her little sister to visit.

It was on one of these visits at the end of May 1883 that she heard of her Uncle James's wish to try for a new position as a groom in Surrey. A clerk in holy orders, 64 year old John Wallace and his wife had returned from an overseas posting and were looking to hire "good hardworking Christian people for positions as groom and housemaid, one child accepted" the advertisement read.

James John and Annie had applied. A young girl was also required to be trained as an under parlour maid. James John thought that the position would suit Lily Mary and had mentioned it to the girl's father. Discussions between Lily Mary's father and uncle became quite heated.

"She should find employment in Whitstable and contribute to the household," fumed her father.

"Be reasonable man! It could be months," argued her uncle, "before she finds a suitable position, there is very little employment locally, you know that."

A decision was made that if James was offered the positions for himself, Annie and Lily Mary, then her father would allow her to go.

"On the understanding," he added, "that part of her wage will be sent home each month to help with the running of the household here in Whitstable."

June passed by with warm hazy days and pale pink sunsets and the air carried the warm sweet scents of summer flowers. Every day Lily Mary hoped that good news from Surrey would arrive. It was mid July and she saw her Uncle just as he turned the corner. Lily Mary lifted her skirts and running as fast as she could, threw herself at him, she had guessed why he was there. He grinned down at his niece.

Leaving Whitstable was not as easy for Lily Mary as she thought it would be. As well as her father and brothers, everyone she had ever known lived here and now it was time to leave them. She consoled herself with the knowledge that at last her dream had come true; she was going to live with her little sister and their uncle.

Her belongings had been taken to James John's house and packed into the travel trunk along with his possessions. After saying her goodbyes to her family, she walked down the narrow road carrying some of her personal items in a small bag, the most important of these being the hairbrush that was her mother's. Many nights Lily Mary would sit holding the brush and imagine her mother's hands once again holding it as she brushed her tight curls.

Lily Mary Mitten. (Photographs by kind permission of Dennis Peto)

Elizabeth Mitten was nearly four years old and had never been away from the little village of Eythorne, so to be riding in a cart being pulled by two horses all the way to Surrey, was a huge adventure to her. Thrushes were singing a song of summer and bumblebees were exploring the flowers at the side of the road. Tiny white clouds floated by in the bright blue sky. What a beautiful day for a new start in life.

The accommodation in Surrey was more than they could have wished for. The Vicarage, nestling in its own wooded grounds, was accessible only by a long sweeping drive. The elegant dining room had a large open fire and high ceilings adding great charm and character to the house. A kindly couple, Mr and Mrs Wallace welcomed the family into their home and showed them to their rooms. In the girls bedroom stood two beds, complete with matching curtains and counterpanes in a soft shade of yellow with a scattering of tiny blue and white flowers. The walls were painted in the palest lemon colour. Lily Mary immediately fell in love with it all and made a vow there and then that when she grew up and had her own house, it would be just like this one. Elizabeth, too young to appreciate the finery of the room just climbed onto the nearest bed and promptly fell asleep.

The adjoining room was for James John and Annie. There were three rag rugs on the floor, one each side of the comfortable looking bed and one in front of the washstand. On this were a matching washbasin and jug, on top of which were two towels, well worn but clean. After putting their belongings down on the floor, James John wrapped his arms around his wife and kissing her cheek told her that he thought that they were going to be so very happy here. Annie looked up at him and smiled in agreement.

Chapter 20

Arthur was released from Kingsnorth School in 1882 and as Rebecca was his next of kin he was released into her care at Eastry. A teenager now, Arthur was a tall, dark, slender boy who never appeared to have any energy, rarely went out and never wanted to mix with the other lads in the village. Kingsnorth Industrial School had certainly changed him.

The following years went by in a seasonal cycles of newborn lambs in spring, suckling and probing their mother's teats whilst their tails wriggled to and fro in a frenzy of delight. Lazy clouds of summer that barely found the energy to move across the bright blue skies. Autumn clouds waved goodbye to a weakening sun as they rushed by on high winds. Carpets of red orange and yellow leaves covered the ground whilst bare trees stood majestically aloof. Winter frost on hedgerows sparkled like a million diamonds under the light of the moon followed by the first falls of snow, which bought the children outside to build snowmen of all shapes and sizes.

Despite his slender build, Arthur had always been healthy but lately had been complaining of feeling unwell. Rebecca had noticed that on some days he hardly touched his dinner when he returned from his work on the farm. He had a cough that would rattle deep in his chest, he became weak and tired.

The homemade cough remedy that she had been administering for the past few weeks was doing Arthur no good at all. After counting the money she had put away for an emergency and deciding the amount would cover his fee, Rebecca decided to call the doctor. She led the doctor up the narrow steep staircase to the small bedroom where her grandson lay.

The room smelt musty and damp, evidence that the household could not afford to light the fires in the bedrooms during the winter months. In one corner there was more proof if more were needed, of how damp the room was. A black patch of mould spread from the ceiling, down the wall and stopped just below the windowsill and the room felt ice cold. The doctor's first thought was that whatever ailed the young man, this room was certainly not going to help his recovery.

Having examined Arthur the doctor followed Rebecca back down stairs and explained, "The boy has tuberculosis, the disease is in its later stages and Arthur is never going to recover. All you can do is to make him as comfortable as possible. Some ethnic minorities are susceptible to this disease, as are people who are malnourished, and although TB is usually spread between members of a family or people who work together, it is also spread very easily in closed spaces over a long period of time especially through people who are or were residents of long-term care facilities including industrial schools."

"Oh no," wept Rebecca, "the poor boy's life has been just awful. I feel as though I am to blame, I should have tried harder with him, then perhaps he would not have ended up in that awful place and caught this disease,"

"You feeling guilty wont change a thing," said the doctor abruptly, "he has TB there is no hope of curing him. I will leave the bill for my visit on the chair here". Picking his hat up off the back of a chair he nodded curtly at Rebecca and let himself out of the house.

Hoping that some warmth would be beneficial to him, Rebecca dragged her grandson's bed downstairs and placed it beside the small fire in the front parlour.

Although money was scarce, even more now that Arthur was unable to work, Rebecca fed him good wholesome food whenever she could. Made sure he had an egg every other day, freshly laid from one of their two hens that had the run of the garden which was situated just beyond the small back yard. She bought cheap cuts of meat, which she diced before putting them in a large pot with an onion, leek or a turnip, a couple of potatoes, a bit of pearl barley, salt, flour and water. "Poor Man's Soup", as it was called, was filling and after a couple of days if extra vegetables were added, the soup would do another days meal. Harriett would help her mother whenever she could but she was the only person working and bringing money into the house so her help was limited to the evening when she would help wash her nephew and straighten his bedclothes. Before going to her place of work each morning Harriett would bring logs in from the yard where they had been chopped and stacked in the summer months,

By the first week in December 1885 Arthur had become skeletally thin, spent days burning with fever followed by nights of shivering sweats, in between which he drifted into restless sleep.

Rebecca would sit by her grandson's bed, listening to him coughing and then crying in pain. Deep in her heart she wished she could just lift the bolster from under his head, smother him and end his pain. He would then be with his mother, something that was denied him for most of his short life. Instead, she brushed the dark curls away from his damp forehead and gently mopped his still handsome face. She gazed at his eyelashes that swept his upper cheeks before curling upwards and at his full thick lips and thought how much he looked like his mother. On good days Arthur would take a few spoonfuls of food and

Rebecca would hope against hope that he would get better, but as the days passed he ate less and less.

Arthur's mouth filled with blood on the morning of Tuesday 22nd December 1885, a few minutes later his suffering ended, his sixteen awful years on earth were over.

Rebecca sat awhile, looking at the lifeless body of her first grandchild while the guilt she had carried for so long washed over her with such force she felt she would drown. Could she have done more for Arthur when he was younger? If she had, would he still have gone to the industrial school? If he hadn't gone to that school would he still have caught the disease that had now killed him?

The ache in her heart made her catch her breath and then the tears came, tears that came from deep inside followed by uncontrollable sobbing. She cried for her grandson, a grandson she both loved and despaired of. Cried for all the times she should have told him she loved him and didn't. Most of all, she cried at the unfairness of it all.

Putting on her thin cloak and boots, she closed and locked the door and started on the short journey to the doctor's house. The wind was blowing an icy chill, a chill that went straight to her bones. Rebecca suddenly realised just how exhausted she was, she struggled to hold herself upright but every so often her shoulders would stoop. Her last meal was two days previously and she hadn't had a decent nights sleep for weeks.

On her return home Rebecca began the task of informing James John, Caroline and Arthur's stepfather that the lad had passed away. She knew they wouldn't attend the funeral due to the wages they would lose if they took time off work.

It didn't really matter, nothing mattered to Arthur now.

It was the day before Christmas. In the middle of the parlour, Arthur as still and cold as marble lay in his coffin, his arms crossed on his chest, coins covering his closed eyelids. Friends and neighbours came to the house to utter their condolences. Some bought a little watery stew, half a loaf and some dripping to spread on it. Other's bought a few logs and other little items, small offerings to see the household through the festive season. Of course there were no decorations festooning Rebecca's mantel shelf. No tree or presents, no meat for Christmas dinner. Nor would there be, how could the traditions of Christmas be celebrated with Arthur's cold, still body lying in the parlour?

Ancient graves crowded Eastry Churchyard, with headstones tilting into each other, others leaning outward as if to hold each other across the tiny path, many of the older ones showing erosion through time and lichen. It was here that Arthur Holder Fitzgerald was laid to rest on Monday the 28th of December 1885.

The lonely figure of his grandmother stood at Arthur's graveside saying her last goodbye, knowing that the memories and echoes he left behind were hers alone to deal with.

Chapter 21

Flags and bunting were going up all over Great Britain. A carnival atmosphere was everywhere in readiness for the Queen's Golden Jubilee Celebrations, one of the greatest events of the Victorian era in Britain. James John, his wife and both nieces, Lily Mary and Elizabeth went to London on June 23rd 1887 and joined the great crowd gathered in Hyde Park in celebration of the 50th year of the reign of Her Majesty Queen Victoria.

What a day they had, and as far as the weather was concerned a hot, sunny one as well. Thousands of youngsters from schools in and around London were entertained in celebration of the occasion. Huge marquees, as well as smaller tents, were pitched on the north-east part of the Park. The children, at a given time and accompanied by their teachers or parents all tucked in to a feast of hams, cheeses, chunks of crusty bread and thick slices of cake. After the food had been eaten there were games to play and attractions to watch just like an enormous fair.

The Lyceum Theatre lent the organisers some kind of mechanical instrument that produced the sound of bells that fascinated the children who had never seen anything like it before. Special issue coins to mark the Golden Jubilee were on display for anyone with enough money to purchase one.

James John and his family could not afford anything as expensive as a coin but there were other souvenirs to commemorate the occasion including teapots, butter dishes, mirrors, handkerchiefs and woven silk pictures. They chose a handkerchief each, including one for Rebecca; they had no real value but it was the memories associated with the souvenirs that gave them value to the family.

Elizabeth was enthralled with everything. She walked between her Aunt and Uncle holding on to one each of their hands, something she would never do in Surrey considering herself at eight years old far too grown up to do such a thing. Here in London though with such large crowds of people milling around she felt it wiser to stay as close to James John and Annie as she possibly could.

A teenager now, Lily Mary was too old to join the children in the marquees but felt very grown up mingling with the crowds of adults. She knew that several of the young men had noticed her good looks, but with a toss of her raven coloured curls she would tilt her head up and pretend she hadn't noticed them.

Then the moment everyone had been waiting for arrived, H.M Queen Victoria. The regimental bands played and the children sang, *"God Bless the Prince of Wales"*, *"God Save the Queen"* and *"The Old Hundredth"* hymn. What a lovely sight and sound it was. For weeks afterwards Elizabeth could talk of nothing else.

Two happy years past, James and his family were still working for Mr and Mrs Wallace and making regular journeys to Kent to visit Rebecca who was now in her 70s. She adored both girls and so looked forward to their visits. She and Lily Mary would talk about work and what plans the young woman had for her future life.

Elizabeth would sit on the floor in front of her Grandmother, staring up at her dark leathery face as she told her of her life with Caesar and of how they came to live in Great Britain. James John noticed the changes in his mother, the girls also commented on the fact that "Grandmother's hands trembled an awful lot sometimes".

A few weeks later came the slowing of her movements, which at first they thought was due to her age but James John had become very concerned about his mother. On their next visit to Kent a few weeks later they noticed that Rebecca was walking with very tiny steps and dragging her right foot. James John thought his mother had suffered a heart attack and asked the doctor to examine her. After seeing Rebecca the doctor informed the family that although she did have a weak heart the cause of her symptoms was Paralysis Agitans and as there was no cure her long term prospects were not good.

"This is a slow progressive disease" the doctor explained, "characterized by a mask-like face with no expression. As the disease invades her body she will have difficulty in moving her arms and legs, they simply will not bend or move and any movement, even attempting to rise from a chair, will not be possible. During the latter stages of this disease your Mother will be unable to swallow."

Three months later Rebecca passed away in the little cottage at Walton, Eastry. The little cottage had been her home for nearly fifty years.

Cottage at Walton.

Chapter 22

For several months Lily Mary had been courting a young man, William Cannings. William worked hard as a carpenter with a local man, spoke with respect to those he came into contact with and was totally in love with Lily Mary as she was with him.

James John and Annie were so pleased when a few months later their niece announced that William had asked to marry her. It felt as though it was their own daughter marrying when they witnessed the happy event. Lily Mary looked beautiful and they were so proud of her. Although only a tiny woman, James John knew she had an inner strength and determination that would serve her well throughout her life. She was a good hard working girl who, in all the years they had cared for her, had not once given him or Annie cause for concern or embarrassment.

Elizabeth however, now she was a very different matter….

A year passed and Elizabeth Mitten, now nearly 14 years old had left school. She had been a very good scholar according to her schoolmistress, had attended every lesson and was polite, well spoken and helpful in class. At home though things were very different, Elizabeth was beginning to give her adoptive parents trouble. They had told her from a very early age about her parentage, thinking it was correct to do so. Now whenever the opportunity arose, the young girl reminded them that they weren't her parents and had no right to tell her what to do. She was insolent and would disobey Annie and James John whenever she could. In an effort to curb these tendencies in her, James John would often resort to using the belt on her backside. This made her even worse. More and more Annie and James John were subjected to Elizabeth's anger and rudeness until one day, when Annie could take no more she threatened to send her to her natural fathers home to live. Elizabeth retorted with a "don't care" that echoed round the house. She then flounced out of the door, slamming it closed behind her.

Crossing over the road she sat in a small wooded area where she and Lily Mary used to go and share their dreams of what their lives would be like when they grew up. Going back to her natural father was never in those dreams, she didn't want to go and live with him. She had met her father only twice, the first time she had been just four years old and didn't really understand that the tall, slim man who had lifted her up and hugged her close to his chest was her father. The second time was at her sisters wedding, to which he had been invited. Father and daughter had spent too many years apart and he was a stranger to Elizabeth, one she didn't particularly like. No, she wasn't going to live with him. She knew though, that in order to stay with James John and Annie she would have to change her ways.

After the death of Mrs Wallace, followed two months later by that of Mr. Wallace, James John and his family, made the journey back to Kent where James John found employment as a gardener in Ramsgate. Both he and Annie loved this area of Kent, an area steeped in history. Ramsgate harbour at was built in 1749 to provide safety for ships seeking shelter. A year later a pier was constructed at the cost of nearly half a million pounds. Later a local carpenter Jacob Steed built timber steps as a way down the cliff face to the harbour below, these steps became known as Jacob's Ladder. In 1846 Ramsgate was linked to South Eastern Railway and with it came more development of the area. James John would often wander down and look across the wide expanse of water, stand awhile and think about his father, and wonder whether it was true that every seagull held the soul of a person lost at sea.

Standing just over 5ft tall Elizabeth was a tiny girl with a slim figure. She possessed a porcelain doll look of fragility, mixed with childlike innocence but she was far tougher than she looked. She was never short of admirers and was a constant source of worry to James John and Annie. She knew the local Ramsgate lads found her attractive and that she could pick whichever one she wanted to if the fancy took her. Instead she liked to flirt and tease them all.

Evening time found her in the park with her friends and after a while the lads, having finished their various work would start drifting in. Elizabeth would sit with her head slightly down and tilted to one side so that her thick hair, the colour of anthracite hung like shimmering curtains partly covering her dark face. As the boys got closer to her she would gaze at them with wide chocolate brown eyes whilst showing pure white teeth between full plump lips. After the lads had shown just enough interest she would throw her head back, her curly hair fanning out like a halo, stand up and walk away giggling to herself. As she walked, she swung her hips so that the boys who were left watching could see every movement of her clothes and could only wonder about the delights that lay beneath. On reaching the park edge that led out onto the narrow pathway, she would lift her skirts just a little too high to be classed as decent, before turning and facing the drooling lads.

Smiling softly she would return home.

Before long, news of Elizabeth's behaviour reached the ears of James John and Annie. They were furious.

"How dare you behave so indecently, that is not the way we have bought you up young lady!" shouted Annie, " if carrying on like that is all you can find to do in your free time, we will find you more chores to do in and around the house."

"You are also forbidden to go anywhere near the park until you know how to conduct yourself," added James John.

Elizabeth promised them that she wouldn't go to the park any more and true to her word she didn't.

She went to the seafront instead.

The local boys soon got to know where she and her friends met and the whole flirting game started all over again. She loved the opposite sex, enjoyed being flirtatious and adored teasing them, no one would change her.

At seventeen years old Elizabeth was working for a local banker, a wealthy man, who was also the head of Ramsgate's social scene. He had four children and a wife who was out most afternoons drinking tea and eating tiny sandwiches with one of her many friends, all of whom wore only the very best jewellery to complement their well-tailored clothes. The banker's home was palatial, filled with crystal glass, exotic carvings complimented by the very best furniture, carpets and tapestries. The front door opened into a huge hall from which a grand marble staircase rose to the upper floor and the sumptuous bedrooms. They enjoyed flaunting their wealth and their ostentatious home meant everything to them.

The running of the house was left to the housekeeper Mrs Ainsley, a sharp nosed, beady eyed woman, with a voice so high pitched some said she could crack glass with it. Her Christian name was Matilda but no one dare call her by her first name, except of course the banker and his lady wife.

The cook Catherine was a large homely woman, with dark blonde hair that had a habit of falling out from under her cap as she worked, and large breasts that seemed to rest on her stomach whenever she sat down.

Elizabeth was the general servant and worked hard six and a half days a week for her employer. Her half-day was the only time she was allowed away from the house and she looked forward to this time a lot. She would sit in her little room on the other six evenings and think "what a waste of time, having to stay in 'just in case she was wanted'".

On Boxing Day 1896 A friend of the banker arrived for a few days break from his business in Ashford.

"The bracing sea air" he told his friend "will do me the world of good after spending fifty weeks of the year stuck in my stuffy solicitors office".

Elizabeth took an instant dislike to the 52 year old, pasty faced, wet lipped man with a belly that hung over the top of his trousers. He however, didn't dislike Elizabeth and made it plain that he could change her life in return for a little kindness.

At home he preached to his wife and children about the virtues of a good Christian family life, but had always had an eye for the ladies and having a "bit on the wrong side of the blanket" was as natural to him as going to Church every Sunday.

"This slip of a girl," he thought gazing at Elizabeth, "would make a welcome bed mate for a while."

Elizabeth certainly wasn't about to be "kind" to him and was pleased when four days later, he returned home.

Spring of 1897 was heralded in with the deep yellow trumpets of daffodils soaking up the pale sun and little green buds that appeared on the once bare branches of the trees. As the evenings grew a little longer Elizabeth, on her half-day off, would take the opportunity to wander down to the beach again, meeting up with friends and the local lads once more. Despite the occasional chill in the evening air, she loved those times, times when the girls would take off their boots and run bare foot across the sand followed by the lads, with others walking or pushing their bikes.

The seaside was a place where social life and simple pleasures for all walks of life was the main attraction. There were ice cream carts standing next to the Punch and Judy shows. Travelling photographers, cockle and mussel stands and sometimes, street musicians, all bustling around on the beach or promenade. The railway, which ran close to the beach, brought single people, parents, grandparents and children for day trips or their annual holiday. Some walked along the promenade taking in the sea air while the wealthier sailed their yachts or rode along the sea front in their carriages. The beach had a strong appeal to Elizabeth and her friends who would sit chatting and watching as the sea lapped at the shore before leaving a ribbon of foam and debris at the tide line. It was here they could relax and their social differences usually went unnoticed.

One Friday evening in May of that year, Elizabeth had decided that she was going to take a walk to the beach, it wasn't her day off, but she couldn't stand being in her pokey little room or sitting in the kitchens for another evening. The banker and his wife had never needed her in the evenings in all the time she had been in their employment. "I might as well go out." she thought, She pulled the back door closed and tiptoed round to the front of the house and through the gate before running down the road towards the beach. Joining her friends, they sat on the sands harmlessly chatting. Telling each other what their days had been like, what latest piece of fashionable clothing they would buy once they had saved enough money, gossiping about who was courting who and what they would do on their day off.

Elizabeth saw him from the corner of her eye as she brushed a strand of hair from her face. She instantly recognised the pasty face. She hadn't known that he was about to visit her employers again and Elizabeth knew that she would lose her job if he went back and told them that she had been out. She was worried now but as he made his way along the road in the direction of Royal Parade and the Paragon, Elizabeth sighed with relief and hoped he hadn't seen her. Half an hour later her crowd of friends began drifting back to their respective abodes, so putting her boots back on Elizabeth set off to her place of work.

She walked up the hill and her heart sank. He was stood just on the corner and Elizabeth had no way off retracing her steps without him seeing her. As she went to pass him, he clasped her arm.

"Well, well," he said with a smug grin, "What are you doing here I thought Sunday was your day off? Do your employers know you are out?"

Elizabeth tried appealing to him, "I have only been out for an hour at the most, just to catch up on the gossip with my friends, we just like to sit and chat."

"That's not what I asked you, is it?" he said, "And I assume that means you have left your place of employment without permission."

Her stomach turned somersaults as she realised that this repugnant man wasn't going let her off that easily. Still grasping Elizabeth's arm he steered her along the road past St. Augustines Abbey on the West Cliff. From there they walked the length of Grange Road until they were a few yards from the entrance to Ellington Park.

The last of the couples that had been for an early evening stroll though the park were now beginning to leave. Ladies in tight fitting jackets, high white collars some with a brooch at the neck, little hats on swept-back hair. Clasping the hand of their lady friends were men in their Norfolk jackets and a straw hat or bowler. Still holding her arm tightly the man ushered Elizabeth towards the darkest part of the park where the trees were thickest and told her what her options were.

"You can," he smirked, "be very, very nice to me and I will ensure your employers are occupied in the drawing room when you return, which will allow you to slip in the back door and up to your room. On the other hand, if you don't want to be nice to me, I will go now and tell them that I have seen their servant on the beach for all to see, behaving as a common prostitute."

She cried her innocence, "I have told you, all we were doing was just talking. We weren't doing anything wrong."

He grinned at her saying, "Your employers will not believe you, I shall make sure of that."

Elizabeth knew what she was expected to do and was mortified; she couldn't imagine anything worse than losing her virginity to a man old enough to be her father.

She woke the next morning feeling sore but with a smile on her face. She didn't like the man, but had liked what he had done to her. Throughout the events of the previous evening he had whispered to her that older men knew how to do things properly. After the second time of making love, Elizabeth thought he could well be right.

Her employer and his lady wife asked her to leave their home as soon as she was unable to carry on with her duties. Elizabeth could have told them that it was their solicitor friend that had fathered her child, but she didn't. She doubted very much that they would believe her anyway. She was now eight months pregnant her belly so swollen that she could barely bend, turning heavy horsehair mattresses and carrying buckets of coal upstairs was just too much for her.

Her first thought was that she should contact James John and Annie and ask to live with them, but then thought better of it. Before she became pregnant they had asked her to visit them on several occasions but after a while they had stopped asking and they had drifted apart. Elizabeth at that time preferred having fun with her friends.

She knew that if she contacted them now they would be horrified at her predicament and no doubt lecture her about her morals.

Chapter 23

The Poor Law Commissioners spent £6,500 building the Isle of Thanet Union Workhouse that was to accommodate 400 inmates. Erected in 1836 on a site at Minster it consisted of a large inner courtyard, which was enclosed by an outer perimeter of drab grey buildings. New arrivals, prior to their formal admission into the main workhouse, would be placed in a receiving or probationary ward. There the workhouse medical officer would examine them and any suffering from an illness would be placed in a sick ward. Their own clothes would be washed and disinfected and then put into store along with any other possessions they had and only returned to them when they left the workhouse.

Elizabeth entered the Workhouse in January 1898, having undergone a lengthy interview by the Master, who deemed that she was in urgent need of admission. Never had she seen so many poverty-stricken people. There were unwanted orphans, impoverished widows as well as those that were just too old to work. There were the sick and deranged, many of whom were walking aimlessly round and round the courtyard uttering inane noises with saliva running down their chins, gazing into space with wild, vacant eyes.

After the admission papers had been dealt with, Elizabeth was presented to the matron and another member of staff in a way that included a racist remark.

"Strip off!" the Matron barked, "Then get yourself washed, and then your hair will be cut and washed in a special solution to ensure that your head lice are eradicated."

"But I bathed this very morning," Elizabeth protested, "and I certainly don't have head lice and never have."

This outburst bought a swift reaction from the matron who grabbed Elizabeth's hair and dragged her to her knees .While the heavily pregnant girl was in that position the matron went though the rules of the workhouse. Elizabeth soon knew the rules by heart as, not only were they displayed on the walls, they were also read aloud every other day so that those inmates who could not read would have no excuses for bad behaviour. Anyone refusing to follow the rules would be severely punished.

Having bathed and had her hair cut, she was then dressed in the Workhouse uniform, and told she would wear a coloured badge to show she was an unmarried mother to be. Her only possessions in the Workhouse were her uniform and the bed she used in the shared dormitory.

Life was meant to be much tougher inside the workhouse than outside and it certainly was. Grey, bare and intimidating the grim buildings housed different classes of inmates who were split into separate areas. Once the inmates were placed on a ward all contact with other classes of inmates was forbidden even at meal times where everyone sat in rows facing the same direction so that no interaction could take place. This awful building housed husbands and wives, who were forbidden to speak to each other and children who went weeks without seeing their parents. Over-crowding and the near starvation diet meant the workhouse was full of illness and disease. The once weekly bath allowed was always supervised which took away every ounce of dignity the inmates may have had left.

In the unlikely event that anyone saw life in the workhouse as an easy option, various forms of labour were organised including breaking stones for use on the roads, chopping logs for firewood and laundry work for the women. Elizabeth soon learnt that although she and all other able bodied people there were expected to work, they would receive no wages as any money made went towards the running of the Workhouse.

It was in that cold, uncaring place on the 15th February 1898 that Elizabeth gave birth to her first child, a girl. She named her Olive because that was the colour of her skin. She had a little screwed up face, which made her skin look as wrinkled as an old lady's, soft black downy hair which curled at her ears and nape of her neck. Large dark brown eyes above a pert button nose and perfectly formed tiny fingers, held clenched into the palm of her little hands. Elizabeth felt a mixture of overwhelming love and pride for the tiny scrap of humanity that she had created.

With this love and pride though, mingled a feeling of dread. She had nothing to offer her child and had no idea where they were going to live. Having seen nothing of James John and Annie she could not turn to them for help. All Elizabeth knew about them was that they were living in a tiny house in St Peters-in-Thanet an area once referred to as "a little island at the end of the world."

Two days after the birth of her daughter, the baby was taken to the children's block and Elizabeth was sent back to work in the laundry.

She argued strenuously that she wanted to keep her baby with her but was told that she was in the Workhouse to obey the rules not make them. Devastated she went about her chores whilst longing to hold her newborn daughter. The rags supplied to Elizabeth by the Matron to use whilst she was menstruating after the birth were as stiff as cardboard and after a few hours Elizabeth could barely walk, the tops of her legs chaffed to a mass of open sores. Every day was one of being shouted at for any small mistake, every meal a tasteless gruel supplemented at times with a piece of bread or a couple of potatoes. Every night was one of broken sleep as women inmates lay on hard beds covered by one thin blanket, sobbing for a husband or child. Elizabeth could take no more of the miserable existence within the walls of the Workhouse and four days later asked to see the Master.

"I can't stay here any longer I want to leave, with my baby," she told him.

"I don't know where you will go," he said, "but as long as you sign your-self out, ensuring that the authorities understand that I did not turn you out, you can go. It makes no difference to me."

"I will sign anything," replied Elizabeth, "if it means I can leave this place."

The following morning the slight, forlorn figure of Elizabeth, trudged towards the outskirts of Ramsgate treading carefully through a layer of newly fallen snow, the baby in her arms shivering and turning blue with the cold.

Knowing that her child needed extra clothing, Elizabeth using the front of her thin-soled boots, scraped a clearing in the snow until she could see small blades of pale green grass. As she laid her in the small clearing, her daughter gasped and shot her tiny arms and legs out as the bitter earth found its way through her thin clothing. Elizabeth quickly took off her own petticoats folded them and wrapped them round her now crying baby. Holding her close so as to keep her warm Elizabeth set off again.

After a few miles she reached a small wood, her feet were aching and it felt as though the sole of her left boot had a hole in it. She stopped and sat beneath a tree, using the trunk to rest her weary back before putting her fretful child to her breast to feed. After her baby had stopped suckling and fallen into what Elizabeth hoped was a deep sleep, she unwrapped the paper from the piece of bread that had been given to her at the Workhouse. The bread was hard and only just edible, but Elizabeth knew that it was all she was likely to get that day.

Her "meal" finished, she carefully folded the paper so she could put it into her boot to cover the hole and make the rest of the journey a little more comfortable. Carefully, so as not to wake the sleeping baby she lent forward and tried to remove her boot which was stuck to her foot, she then realised that her feet had been bleeding. If she took her boot off now, she had no doubt that she would never get it back on again and decided to leave well alone. Having brushed the snow from her clothes she carried on towards her uncle James home, praying that he and Annie would not turn her away.

Annie had laid more logs on the fire and was putting away the crockery when she heard a timid knock on the door. She hardly recognised her adopted daughter who, although only twenty years old looked so much older. She was thin, her once beautiful hair looked awful poking out from under her bonnet at all angles, her hands were so cracked they had started bleeding and her eyes had lost their sparkle. Taking the sleeping baby from Elizabeth's arms, Annie called to her husband, "Look who has come back home."

James John gave Elizabeth a hug and kissed the top of her head, then knelt in front of her and helped her remove her boots. There were blisters of all sizes, some filled with fluid, others broken and raw with flaps of skin through which bright red patches of flesh could be seen. Filling an old pan with tepid water and a sprinkling of salt, he placed it on the floor in front of her and told Elizabeth to soak her feet. Elizabeth could not control her emotions any longer. Embarrassment and tiredness, overwhelming her, she buried her head in her hands and sobbed.

"No crying now, Elizabeth, the time for tears is over," he said kindly, "You and the baby are more than welcome to stay here, you should know that."

"Oh thank you Uncle," sobbed Elizabeth, "I will try my hardest to find a job and repay you and Aunt Annie for all you are doing for me."

"We don't want payment, just find employment and provide for you and the baby; you can live here rent free. All we ask in return is that you start to act responsibly and bring no further shame into our house. Now, tell us everything that has happened to you."

Whilst Elizabeth was telling them of her life since they last saw each other, Annie opened the large box that doubled as a seat under the parlour window. Inside, clean and neatly folded were all the baby clothes that Annie had bought for Elizabeth when she was a baby.

"Although these are old, I think Olive will look just beautiful in these," Annie said, handing the bundle to Elizabeth, "I had saved them for when James John and I had a baby, but sadly that is never going to happen now."

The following day, Elizabeth was out looking for work and continued to do so until she was finally hired as a laundress. There were eight people in the household and the work was hard, but at least the Master allowed her to take Olive with her.

By the end of the week, Elizabeth was so tired she could hardly turn the handle of the heavy mangle that squeezed the water from the clothes. When the weather was wet the clothes were hung from a wooden frame suspended from the kitchen ceiling to dry. The oil lamps and candles that lit the house soon made the washing a dirty grey colour, when the weather was better, the freshly laundered clothes were hung outside but before long it was speckled with chimney soot from the coal fires. Anything white, like tablecloths didn't stay white for long. It was a heartbreaking job, but a job and for that Elizabeth was grateful. She was happy now and it showed in the way she was content just to stay in of an evening and be with her daughter. As the months went by, Olive continued to grow into a strong healthy baby with a ready smile for everyone and Elizabeth took great delight in showing her off and could think of nothing that could mar her happiness. How wrong she was.

On the 2nd of September 1898, Olive had been given her breakfast and placed in her baby carriage, a few minutes later the baby's screams bought the adults rushing to her side. It was just a bit of diarrhoea and not much to worry about thought Annie and voiced her opinion to Elizabeth. A week later on the 6th September, Elizabeth gave her daughter the medicine that the she had bought from the doctor, before laying her daughter in the big armchair by the window while she collected water and a rag to wash her with. When she returned from the scullery, Olive was dead.

Elizabeth knew only too well that she came from a walk of life far lower than many but, she thought, no parent should have to sit and cradle the lifeless body of their child, a child who was supposed to have outlived them. In the distance she could hear someone screaming and calling for Annie and James John. It was her.

Chapter 24

By November 1899 Elizabeth knew that she was pregnant again but managed to hide her condition from both her employer and her family under layers of winter clothing. With the coming of spring 1900 and the first spell of warmer weather, Elizabeth could no longer hide her condition under her winter clothes.

Annie was at the window admiring the columbine that had just started to flower and the other plants that were coming alive again with fresh green leaves. She saw Elizabeth walk up the short path to the front door and she instinctively knew.

That evening James John told Elizabeth that he would make arrangements for her admittance into the workhouse, he also added that when she was released he would prefer her not to return to his home. He loved the girl he had raised as his own, but it was time she took responsibilities for her actions.

Elizabeth sat with her head in her hands, not really believing that she was pregnant and back in the workhouse again. She had grieved for her first born by working hard in the beginning, but after a while, when the pain inside her had eased she had returned to her old ways of going out with her friends, male and female.

James John and Annie had both told her that they would not have her in their home should she bring any more shame upon them. Elizabeth had assured them that she had learnt from her past mistake and would not get pregnant again. The truth was that there were so few pleasures that the lower class could afford that Elizabeth and many others like her, helped themselves to the one they enjoyed most.

The workhouse was just as she remembered it, drab and depressing, filled with people who had become drab and depressed, of which she was one again. Young children, ill with whooping cough, diarrhoea and measles, and respiratory diseases such as pneumonia and bronchitis took their grim toll on all age-groups. On her admission papers she gave her name as Bessie in the hope that the Master would not remember her. Unfortunately he remembered her only too well. Who could forget the stubborn, argumentative slip of a girl with the near black skin, black hair and a face that would make men go weak at the knees. Once the Matron learned that Elizabeth had been in the workhouse just over a year previously, the racist name-calling began and once again Elizabeth's life was pure misery.

Hilda was born in May 1900, just as beautiful as her sister had been, with the same soft skin, little button nose and big brown eyes. Elizabeth worried every day about her baby, she didn't want to let her out of her sight for fear of history repeating itself and another child dying. Working long hours in the laundry she longed for the days to end so she could see her daughter.

Three days later back at his home in St Peters, James John heard of a recently bereaved widower, George Hatcher who lived in Kent. His elderly sister lived in the same little row of cottages as James John.

"George is finding things very difficult, trying to work and look after his four youngest daughters who are between seven and 12 years old," she explained, "his eldest daughter has given up work and is acting as housekeeper for him, but she is planning to get married in the near future and will soon be leaving home. I'm nearly 63 years old, it would be too much for my old bones to offer any help to my brother."

"I have," she continued, "taken the liberty of explaining Elizabeth's delicate situation to George and asked him whether Elizabeth might be a suitable person to help look after his children and the house. George warmed to the idea immediately and said that if Elizabeth accepted the job, he would pay a small wage and provide a warm secure home for her and the baby."

James John made arrangements with the workhouse to visit Elizabeth one evening and was shocked to see how tired and drawn she looked. She heard his voice and looking up from her sewing she smiled a smile that said she was so very pleased to see him.

James John put his arm round her shoulder and whispered, "I didn't mean the things I said, you know that don't you?"

Elizabeth put her hand on his and gently squeezed it, "I don't blame you for what was said, I deserved it. I really am sorry for everything I have put you and Annie through, I'm so glad you have forgiven me. By the way, how did you manage to arrange a visit with me at this time of night? Is Annie unwell?"

"Annie is fine," explained James John. "I just have something to tell you."

The tale of George Hatcher had barely left his lips, when Elizabeth told James John she would love to look after his children and would sign herself out of the workhouse as soon as she could. The next afternoon, James John returned to the Workhouse with a cart in which he had loaded Elizabeth's small cast iron bed, bedding, a chamber pot and the few other belongings she had accumulated while living at St. Peters.

After helping Elizabeth and her baby into the cart, he flung her small bag of possessions in after her.

Elizabeth felt a mixture of excitement and fear during the journey to Ash. Excitement as this was the first day of her new life, where if she continued to work hard and keep away from the many men who swarmed round her, would be a life of some security. The fear she felt was of the unknown, she had never met Mr. Hatcher and wondered whether he would find her suitable to look after his children. She needn't have worried. On reaching the house, the door opened and George Hatcher a tall, swarthy skinned man with a huge bushy beard and deep brown eyes smiled down at her. His children were standing just behind him, all looking as nervous as Elizabeth felt. George invited the weary travellers into his home and after introducing everyone asked his daughter Kate, to show Elizabeth up to the room that would be hers and baby Hilda's.

Kate was 20 years old, one year younger than Elizabeth and by the time the two of them returned to the front parlour, they were chatting like old friends. Kate explained that she was due to marry in a few weeks time and would be moving away from the area which would mean there would be no one to keep house and care for her siblings. She was so glad that Elizabeth had agreed to take on the job.

James John kissed Elizabeth goodbye, thanked George for the tea he had offered, turned and quickly walked down the path to the waiting horse and cart and began his journey home.

Chapter 25

Life for Elizabeth and the Hatcher family was much the same as any other household in the small community. The day began at 4.30 am and finished when the last of the children were tucked up in bed. Six weeks after Elizabeth's arrival at the Hatcher family home, Kate left to be married. The summer of 1900 passed with the weather acting as it usually did, temperatures reached 31°C in London on the 11th of June but other areas had severe thunderstorms with many people being hurt by hailstones that dropped from the sky like marbles.

From the end of September, once the children were in bed and asleep George would spend many hours a week in the small scullery. On the cold stone floor he would chisel, hammer, smooth and paint chunks of wood, which he would transform into toys. A croquet set, dominoes and bagatelle. A Noah's ark complete with a selection of animals for baby Hilda, who he thought of as his own. On his farm labourer's wage he could not afford any fancy shop bought toys. While the scullery was being used as a make-shift carpenters shop, Elizabeth busied herself in the parlour and by Christmas morning the girls all had one toy, a red velvet skirt and an apple all tucked into the pillow case they had hung at the end of the mantelpiece the night before. Elizabeth had made the skirts from old curtains she had found in one of the shops in Sandwich. In the same shop she had bought a few remnants of different coloured ribbons and lace that she had sewn onto the skirts, so making each one individual.

Sprigs of holly with its red berries and dark green spiky leaves that Elizabeth and the children had collected from the lanes adorned the parlour. Elizabeth explained "The prickly leaves of the holly represent the crown of thorns that Jesus wore when he was crucified and the berries, drops of blood shed by Him because of the thorns."

Christmas dinner was carrots and mashed potato with pork from the pig killed by the farmer for whom George worked. The pork dripping was spread on bread for breakfast long after Christmas had gone.

The last day of 1900 was spent like any other. George went to work at 5.30am while Elizabeth began the weekly wash, after which she cleaned the little house of the dust that had gathered over the Christmas period and cooked the potatoes that would be served with the cold meat and pickles for dinner that evening.

By 9 o'clock that evening, George was in the local Inn awaiting the arrival of the New Year with his work friends. Back at his house the children were all in bed and asleep, two loaves of bread were baking in the oven and Elizabeth decided to have her weekly bath to rid her body of the smell of hard work. Putting the two big pans of water onto the fire to heat she went upstairs and collected her soap and towel. Back downstairs she went outside, lifted the small tin bath from the hook at the side of the house and dragged it into the scullery. After pouring the warm water from both pans into the bath, Elizabeth refilled them and placed them back on the fire. Undressing and stepping into the water which barely covered her buttocks, Elizabeth started washing her hair by tipping water from a pan over it, rubbing it well with the fancy soap that had been her Christmas present from the Hatcher family. Having rinsed her hair she stepped out of the bath to get a fresh pan of water from the fire.

George decided he would go home and tell Elizabeth that after the Inn had closed its doors for the evening, he would be bringing his workmates home for a small tot of hot rum to help the New Year in and would she make sure the fire was banked up before she went to bed.

Opening the door to the scullery George stood quite still, unable to take his eyes off of her. The beads of water, clinging to her firm lithe body shone like sparkling diamonds in the flickering candlelight. He could see the faint glow of the fires dying embers on her dark skin, skin that was as smooth a satin. Her dark hair hung past her shoulders in a tumble of wet raven coloured curls. She turned towards him, unashamed of her nakedness, her eyes flashed with a hundred smiles and thousands of tantalizing promises. He ran his hand through her wet hair, moving it off of her shoulder and exposing one of her pert breasts. A thrill ran down her spine and she closed her eyes. In one movement he had taken her into his arms. She was soft and warm and smelled faintly of fresh baked bread and apple blossom soap. George knew that she must have been with many different men, but she was his now and oh, how he adored her.

The wedding invitations George and Elizabeth sent were very formal and very few. Not engraved invitations on smooth, medium weight pure white paper that the upper classes could afford, but hand written by Elizabeth on paper that was thin and ivory coloured. On the bottom of each invitation she had added a little monogram, her initials entwined with George's.

They were married on June 15th 1901 at Woodnesborough, Kent. George was nearly 56 years old, Elizabeth was 21. Her wedding band was made to form two hands clasped together, a symbol of unity. It didn't matter to her that it was an old ring, she thought it was beautiful. The traditional wedding march *"Here Comes the Bride, (all dressed in white)"* didn't apply to Elizabeth having already had two children.

"Anyway, what a terrible waste of money," she exclaimed "to buy a fancy white dress just to wear once"

Instead she wore her best outfit, a light brown gored skirt and white blouse which Elizabeth had edged with a delicate piece of lace at the neck and cuffs. Over these she wore a hip-length cloak, just perfect to disguise the fact that she was pregnant again. She carried her old Bible and a tiny posy of white flowers the stems of which she had tied with a satin ribbon. The couple had a tea reception in the late afternoon with their children, a few neighbours, James John and Annie, who had made the wedding cake and Lily Mary and her husband who provided the finger sandwiches and scones with jam.

Three months later their son Percival George was born. Life was quite good for George and Elizabeth at this point in their lives. They had a reasonable wage coming into the house, due to the long hours that George worked, so their table was never bare.

One by one during the next seven years, the girls that Elizabeth had been employed to care for left home, all had found jobs which required them to live-in and as each girl left home, George and Elizabeth had another baby. Baby Lillian Agnes, was followed by Irene Rose and then Florence Elsie. All had inherited Elizabeth's dark skin, black curly hair and chocolate brown eyes.

With an ever growing family to feed George worked as many hours as he could, he was the only wage earner and the weekly expenditure since the arrival of the children would more often than not exceed the weekly wage. Most vegetables were grown in the tiny garden at the rear of the house, the whole family lending a hand to turn the soil and break the clods of earth. In order to "acquire" the seed potatoes he needed,

George stealthily walked the fields at dusk after the farmers had lifted their crop, his keen eyes searching out the small potatoes that had been left lying in the fields. These he put in old boxes, covered with a sack and slid underneath the bed he shared with Elizabeth. After a while these same potatoes had strong white shoots growing from them. Soon it was time to plant them, which was the job of the older children who planted each one about a foot apart. George would "bank them up" with the freshly turned soil. He "acquired" most of his other vegetables in the same way. Whenever the farmer's fields were fully planted with cabbage, beet, onion or turnip, George, after leaving the inn would go for an evening stroll, returning home with young, freshly pulled plants. Some he would shove into the pockets of his coat, others would be put down the leg of his trousers, the bottom of which he tied tight with string. The following evening the plants would be replanted in the Hatchers little vegetable garden. He never acquired too many and was never greedy, he just wanted enough to feed his family.

Elizabeth too, soon learnt how to economize and became an expert on using scraps of food to make a filling meal. Before boiling the carcass of a chicken that had been part of the previous days dinner, she would very carefully pick off every particle of meat, to this she would add some dripping. Into a stew pan she put an equal measure of milk and water, a good-sized chopped onion and slices of diced turnip. This was simmered until the milk tasted strongly of the onions after which the liquid was poured into a small jug. A piece of lard was put in the stew pan with the onions and turnip pulp and once the lard had melted, flour was added. This done, the flavoured milk and water mixture was poured into the pan and once it had slightly cooled, the chopped meat was stirred in. Once the mix was completely cold, it was shaped into small sized balls, which were fried in dripping and served with boiled potatoes.

Their "summer holiday" was a walk to the seaside where the girls tucked their dresses into their drawers and with Percy, paddled in the water while the wet sand pushed up through their toes or sat and watched the donkeys walking slowly up and down the beach, each with a young passenger on it's back. There was always a small ice cream for eating on the walk home and the children would talk about it for days afterwards. Some weeks if there was a few pence over after everyone had been fed and worn clothes replaced, George and Elizabeth would treat themselves to the "luxury" of ¼ oz of tobacco.

She loved her home, but sometimes Elizabeth wished that she had been born or married into the middle or upper classes. Their homes were larger, better built and had most of the new gadgets installed such as inside bathrooms and toilets, even gas lighting. Some had water pumps in their kitchens or sculleries and their waste was taken away into underground sewers. Stylish flowery wallpaper adorned the walls and heavy curtains hung at every window, keeping out the winter chill. These people had rugs and carpets, fancy ornaments from expensive London shops or from far away lands.

Come evening time though, when the last of the children were in bed, she and George would sit at the old table in the scullery, telling each other the latest village gossip or laughing at what one of the children may have said and Elizabeth would stop envying the rich for what they had. She had what she wanted all under the roof of this tiny cottage.

George first complained of feeling unwell in January 1913. Gradually his strength started to fail, slowly he all but stopped eating and his once upright muscular body became thin and stooped. He was the only breadwinner and being in bad health was a constant fear of his, he knew without doubt that he was not well now, but he had to keep working or it would mean the workhouse for the entire family. Sadly it was only a matter of time before he could no longer work and the family were to be evicted from the cottage that went with his farm job. Both George and Elizabeth pleaded with the farmer, "Please let us stay, all we are asking for is a few more weeks grace."

"Look," said the farmer, "it's July, one of the busiest times of the farming year. George's job has already been taken and the new farm labourer is waiting to move into the cottage. There is nothing I can do for you."

At that moment George knew that the workhouse was the only option open to them.

Elizabeth became hysterical, "I have had first hand experience of life in the workhouse and I just can't bear the thought of having to enter one again," she cried. "When I close my eyes I still have images in my mind of those poverty-stricken, unwanted people, many of them too old to work or sick and deranged. All of us packed together in the workhouse in a ruthless attempt to solve the problem of us poor. I would do anything, anything at all rather than enter the workhouse again."

"What do you expect me to do?" said George weakly, "I can't help being ill."

"Just do something," Elizabeth spat.

Too tired to even answer, George sat down, his shoulders slumped forward and a long sigh escaped his lips.

Later that evening, when George and the children were in bed, sleeping, Elizabeth left the house and walked to a cottage half a mile away to beg the help of a widower friend of George's, a man by the name of Richard Saxby.

"Richard, could you please find it in your heart to put me and the children up for a few days?" she begged. "George is going into the workhouse tomorrow and I have to leave the house, I just don't know what's to become of us. It won't be for long, when George is well enough he will come home and then find another farm job."

Richard readily agreed.

The next morning, twelve years of memories, smiles and tears, love and anger left with George and Elizabeth as the door to the cottage was locked firmly by the farmer at 6am on 29th May 1913. George by this time was very ill and on reaching Eastry Workhouse collapsed just inside the entrance from where he was taken immediately to the hospital block.

This was to become the final "home" for a man who had worked hard all his life, had fed and clothed nine children and was loved and respected by all of them. He had asked for nothing from anyone. The doctor finished his examination of George and in the medical officers book wrote, *"Carcinoma of the stomach. Unfit. To be given sick diet."*

At the home of Mr. Saxby, called Hamill Cottage in Woodnesborough, Kent, Elizabeth and her children were living in one tiny bedroom. There was hardly any room to move in such a small area and after one week of sleepless nights, it was decided that Elizabeth slept down stairs in one of the large, stained and well-worn chairs. Percy, who was now 12 years old, would sleep in Mr. Saxby's bedroom on a sack filled with straw while the three girls, Lillian, Irene and Florence would share a bed upstairs. Hilda their older sister had already found a live-in job as a scullery maid at Lydd, Kent.

Two fraught filled weeks passed. There was never enough food for all the mouths that Hamill Cottage now held and Richard was becoming irritable with the petty quarrelling that goes hand in hand with young siblings. He was 59 years old and thought his days of having a house full of young children were a thing of the past. He didn't dislike them but they weren't his flesh and blood. Elizabeth, who had not had a decent nights sleep since arriving at the cottage, felt that she could not go on. Her hands were sore and bleeding where the rough handle of the hoe rubbed as she weeded the field of young plants, a job offered by the local farmer and one that she knew she could not refuse. She still had her four children to feed and clothe and was trying so hard to keep her family together. Although only in her early thirties she began to take on the haggard, worn look of someone much older.

Every now and then, anger at what life had dealt her simmered within her body. When the simmering reached boiling point her anger would explode into an uncontrollable rage, with her children on the receiving end. Afterwards, when she saw the awful marks she had inflicted on them, her tears would flow and she would hold her young ones while trying to explain that she hadn't meant to hurt them.

Elizabeth collapsed in July 1913. The combination of grief on hearing that George was so ill and would not be coming out of the workhouse and exhaustion from long hours of back breaking work had finally taken its toll. Richard sat with her until she had recovered.

Looking at Lillian he said, "Pour your mother a strong cup of tea from the pot that's stewing on the grate, put plenty of sugar in it."

Lillian dutifully did as she was told and gently stroked her mothers arm as she handed her the tea.

"Right, you children, go to your bedroom," Richard ordered, "I want to speak to your mother alone."

Half an hour later they heard Richard calling them and one by one four bewildered children entered the small parlour. Just the sight of their mother was enough to tell the older two Percy and Lillian, that something awful was about to happen and instinctively they put a protective arm around Irene and Florence.

Chapter 26

Eastry Union Workhouse was erected in the 1830s in Mill Lane and was designed to cater for about 550 inmates. To the north of the site was the entrance block while around a large courtyard a few two-storey blocks were built. In 1871 fever wards were built south of the workhouse.

A large chapel stood within the workhouse grounds where morning and night, prayers were said and a service took place twice every Sunday. Workhouse discipline was extremely severe and it was rumoured that in one such place a nine year old girl, after committing a minor offence was locked in the mortuary for a night with a corpse. The Master and Matron were subsequently dismissed after an enquiry was held into their conduct.

The workhouse diet was repetitive and unappetizing, for breakfast porridge made from water was supplemented with bread. Dinner consisted of meat and potatoes: meat was usually cheap cuts of beef or mutton, with occasional pork or bacon, usually boiled. For variation, once a week fish would be served. Broth, which was served at supper was usually the water used for boiling the dinner meat, with a few turnips, carrots and onions added.

In the Admission and Discharge Register for Eastry Workhouse the required information was entered:

Percy

Lillian

Irene

Florence

Saturday 19th July 1913. Children of George Hatcher a Farm Labourer admitted from St Peter, Church of England, Sandwich.

Name and address of nearest relative:

Elizabeth Ann Hatcher. Mother.

C/o Mr. Saxby, Hamill Cottage, Woodnesborough, Sandwich.

As she was leaving Elizabeth smiled at her children, kissed them all one by one and said, "You will be coming home very soon."

Percy and Lillian knew otherwise.

"No we won't," replied Percy, "I just know we won't."

"Just tell us the truth Mother," begged Lillian.

Age twelve and ten years old respectively, they knew their mother was lying.

"Your father is only in the next block," she said, "you may be able to see him every day but I have to go now, look after Irene and Florence wont you."

She closed her ears to the heart wrenching cries of her children and walked away knowing that the rest of their childhood would be characterised by gruelling hardship and responsibility thrust upon their young shoulders.

The four Hatcher children stood in the receiving ward while a medical officer examined them for any illnesses. After being stripped and bathed they were then given workhouse clothes to wear, blue and white striped dresses, black stockings and black boots for the girls. For Percy, corduroy trousers, a thick grey flannel shirt, black socks and hobnailed boots. All made from coarse hard-wearing materials and designed to be practical rather than comfortable.

One of the first lessons the Hatcher children learnt in the workhouse was that "crying is not allowed". They immediately dried their tears whilst being watched over by a very stern matron. Confusion filled their minds. Why were they in here? Why did their mother not love them? What had they done wrong? Did Hilda know where they were? Four more poor children to add to the already large number, condemned to spend part or all of their childhood within the walls of the workhouse.

It was here within the workhouse walls that the overseers hoped to *"form the character of the children here, so that their lives maybe industrious, orderly and sober because the peace and safety of the whole village depend upon the habits and character of the poor"*.

Sunday school teachers were told to *"use any means to stop the rudeness in any of the children's manners as well as the disgusting obscenity of their language. To make sure the children were taught to be honest, obedient, courteous, industrious and submissive in order to change the whole character of the lower classes."*

Dinner was first meal for the Hatcher children in the workhouse, after which the girls watched as their brother was marched away to the boy's block.

A week later in the Register of Deaths for Eastry Union the Doctor wrote;

George Hatcher, age 69 years. Died on 23rd July. Was admitted from the parish of Woodnesborough and buried by friends.

The Hatcher children didn't know it, but their beloved father was dead and no one bothered to tell them.

As the weeks passed and turned into months, several attempts were made to return the girls to their Mother who by this time had married Richard Saxby but they were returned to the workhouse after each attempt, all of them being found wandering the streets begging, underfed, without shoes and dirty. People in the little village shunned her for not caring for her children and Elizabeth knew she was doing wrong, but she would not allow her children to interfere with her new life.

Unable to persuade their Mother to change her ways the four children were taken into the care of the workhouse guardians who reported:

"The opinion of the guardians is that the mother is "immoral". She herself has borne two illegitimate children and her disgusting behaviour when with her children gives rise for concern for said children. Of course the colour of her skin is testimony enough to her lack of morals in regard to herself and her children. It has been noted many times that the morals of these people are considerably lower than our own. Having heard of their mothers neglect to provide for these children, it is undesirable that she should have control of them.

Their natural home, such as it is, being the worst place for them, it is our responsibility now to safeguard, protect and manage the interest of these children by removing them from such awful immoral surroundings.

The Hatcher children will become wards of the state, either here in the workhouse, in industrial schools or wards of private charities, such as the Waifs and Strays Society. We hope we have intervened in time to stop these children following in their mother's ways."

Chapter 27

The Hatcher children, now under the care of the guardians, their hair cropped short and heavy thick soled boots encasing their feet, along with the other workhouse children were marched to school in twos, crocodile fashion, with the shouts and laughter of the village children echoing in their heads. It was no use trying to hide their faces. This would be met by a sharp slap across the back of the head by a member of the workhouse staff. They just had to walk on for all to see. The knowledge that they were "different" to the other children was painful enough for them; the poverty added insult to injury.

Nearly three years later in February 1916, unbeknownst to his sisters, Percy was sent into service with a Mr. Petit at Ware Farm in Ash. Four weeks later Mr. Petit and Percy visited the workhouse governor

Sitting at his huge desk the governor listened as Mr Petit explained, "I would very much like to keep this boy in my employ, having found him to be very satisfactory during the month's trial. He is a hard worker, eager to learn new skills and is also polite."

The Governor looked over the top of his spectacles at Percy.

"Well boy," he asked kindly, "what say you? Do you like living and working at the farm?"

"Oh yes Sir, I do," replied Percy.

"Are you cared for and treated well?" questioned the governor.

"Extremely well sir, I am very happy there".

Half an hour later with the necessary paperwork signed, Percy without a backward glance, left the workhouse for the last time.

Lillian was sent to St Helen's Orphanage at Ipswich, Suffolk, which was run as a Girls Training Home on 23rd March 1916, followed two months after by Irene.

The effect on Florence was catastrophic. She was just nine years old, her sisters were the only family she could remember, the only ones who would put a comforting arm around her when the jibes about her colour became too much to bear. How she wished she could answer her tormentors back but she was just too timid. She would scurry along; head bowed and try to close her ears to the taunts of "woolly head", "nigger" or "coon". Her sisters had known how to handle those that had tormented them. They had held their heads up high, as if they were royalty even though they were dressed in rags and fixed the tormentors to the spot with just a stare. Florence knew she would have to learn to do the same. The young girl felt so lonely, out of reach of any love or affection with no friends and her sisters gone. When she wasn't busy in the laundry, Florence would spend her time staring out of the window at the empty road below, like a trapped bird in a cage. She seemed to cope with being tormented throughout the day but during her sleeping hours her dreams turned into nightmares.

For Lillian and Irene life in the Training School proved to be just as grim as the workhouse. Both had to work hard, rising at quarter to six in the morning, their beds had to be made with each corner of the paper thin mattress perfectly squared by the stiff unyielding sheet. It was then time to scrub and polish the vast area of floor space before sitting down on hard benches for the first of their tasteless meals. Every day, for at least three hours, they were taught reading, writing and the principles of Christianity so that they would become useful and virtuous adults. After dinner they scrubbed cutlery, pots and pans which had to be clean and shining. At evening time they would sit on wooden benches patching and darning their clothes. When they could no longer darn their stockings they spent the evenings knitting more, having been told *"Don't just sit there, get you're knitting out, you know the Devil finds mischief for idle hands."*

Open air games or activities were unheard of except for a brisk walk round the gardens each day, they rarely ventured outside the grounds as the upper class residents complained to anyone that would listen, that the girls were lowering the moral tone of the area.

St Helens was their home for nearly three years before Lillian and Irene were returned to Eastry Workhouse in November 1919. Both girls were so looking forward to meeting with their younger sister again and had often spoken about what she would look like now she was twelve years old and nearly grown up. Lillian broke down in tears on being informed that her baby sister had been removed from the workhouse a year earlier. The authorities wouldn't even tell her where Florence was; saying only *"We are under no obligation whatsoever to tell you anything. Florence had been misbehaving and is now boarded out in another institution".*

December of that year was an extremely cold month with north-easterly winds, coupled with a severe gale in Kent. Parts of the southeast had no sun at all in the first ten days and the girls felt as miserable as the weather was. Hope was the only thing that kept them sane, hope that one day they would leave the workhouse and be re-united with their little sister and older brother. They would whisper of the things they would do when they were free of the workhouse, of the fine clothes they would wear and of the posh houses they would live in. Silly hopes and dreams of young girls, but hopes and dreams that made long bleak days pass just a little quicker.

In celebration of the fast approaching Christmas period the Master informed the inmates that he would allow the dinner hall to be decorated. By Christmas Eve, it was tastefully dressed with holly sprigs and evergreen. One of the older women made a holly wreath that was placed over the doorway of the hall. On Christmas morning everyone was allowed an extra quarter of an hour in bed after which they gathered in the hall for breakfast. As usual the food of porridge, bread and butter followed by a mug tea was eaten in silence. By ten o'clock the able bodied were assembled in the dining hall again, for the choral service officiated by the local vicar. The hall rang out with the words of *"Hark the Herald Angels Sing"* Among the singing, stifled sobs could be heard, sobs that told the misery of the workhouse children who so wanted to be at home for Christmas. Sobs of the mothers who wished they could have afforded just a small gift for their children and the sobs of Lillian and Irene for their youngest sister.

The service over, the inmates were allowed to spend an hour in the dormitories but by 1pm the dining-hall was crowded again for the most important part of the day, Christmas dinner. To the inmates, with their bland weekly diet, Christmas was looked forward to as a brief spell of joy and one good dinner. This comprised of thinly sliced roast beef, mashed potatoes, followed by plum pudding which was in complete contrast to the suet pudding or bread and soup which would otherwise have been the main meal of the day. Tea was at five thirty, consisting of cheese, bread and butter, cake and tea and was enjoyed by everyone.

Chapter 28

In January 1920 Lillian who was now seventeen years old was discharged from the workhouse, working instead for the workhouse as a domestic servant at the sanatorium.

She was back in the workhouse after only two weeks having been dismissed for being "aloof, uncooperative and unnecessarily stubborn". Lillian continued with these traits. When spoken to in a civil manner, she would respond in the same way and would work hard and with a thoroughness that surprised even the matron, who would run a finger over the tops of doors in search of a speck of dust. Speaking to Lillian as if she was the lowest of the low brought out a totally different person. She would turn the most simple of tasks into a whole afternoon's work; even then the job would not be done properly. She endured punishment after punishment. Her leisure time was stopped, she was deprived of her evening meal or made to rise and start work an hour earlier than the other inmates.

Whatever punishment was metered out, it made no difference. Lillian reasoned that it was not her fault that she was in the workhouse, so she shouldn't be spoken to in the same manner as one would speak to a dog. She also stressed to Irene that she shouldn't let people speak to her as if she was a nobody.

Before long the authorities forbade any contact between the two sisters and placed them in different dormitories. Still it made no difference. If Lillian decided she wished to see her sister, she would ignore the shouts of the master, stride off, head held high in search of Irene. Several times the master would try to restrain her, calling for help from other staff members but Lillian would carry on walking. Her inner strength fuelled by anger. They were not going to stop her seeing her sister. During the next three months Lillian received every form of punishment there was. Her attitude remained the same, stubborn. It was decided that the only way to control the Hatcher girls was to place them in separate counties until they both left the care of the workhouse guardians.

On 21st April 1920 Irene was sent to St Edith's Home in Fareham, Hampshire. This home was built in 1884 but when the old premises became "too old for repair" a new Home was built and renamed St Edith's Home for Girls, dedicated by the Bishop of Southampton on July 19th 1907. Throughout this time St Edith's was almost entirely self-supporting, living from the profit made from the girls' work in laundry and needlework.

This was Irene's home until two years later when she found full time employment and later still, a husband.

Lillian was removed from Eastry and sent to the Girls Training Home at Chatham which was established in the mid 1800's for the sole purpose of taking in "fallen" or "difficult" girls.

Once there, Lillian was interviewed while notes were made about her fall into delinquency, her mental condition, education, ambitions and failures. Notes were also made on whether she could be trusted around men or boys and if she was prone to pilfering.

The admission document, duly signed by the Training Home Governors, was handed to Superintendent so allowing

Lillian to be admitted. She bought with her as requested by the home; two pairs of shoes, four pocket-handkerchiefs, two petticoats, two nightgowns, three vests, three pair of knickers, two pair of stockings, brush and comb in a bag and a toothbrush.

Lillian was the placed in the probationary block where she stayed for three weeks as a precaution against bringing any diseases into the home after which the daily monotonous routine began. Prayers were said at 6.00 every morning before breakfast was eaten in the dining room at 7.30. After breakfast there were various domestic duties to perform. Like the other girls there, Lillian was trained once more for work in the laundry, the Home providing a full washing and ironing service for the local people. None of the girls received a wage or even spending money for this heavy, backbreaking, manual work. A ten minute break was allowed at mid morning and again in the afternoon, dinner was at 1 o'clock. At 6.30 sharp supper was eaten, followed with prayers at 7.30 and a brief recreational period before bed at 9pm.

As well as discipline there was also fun times and the girls played cards, knitted and sang songs, Lillian also learnt to dance and play the piano. She was a popular young lady, who despite, or maybe because of what life had dealt her, had a wonderful sense of humour.

When the time came for leaving the home the girls were found jobs by the superintendent, always as domestic servants. They were bought up to be servants, their class and gender having restricted their lives.

Chapter 29

Elizabeth Hatcher had married Richard Saxby, not a cruel man but a hard one, nine months after she had placed her children in the workhouse and now had three other small children. She had no idea though of the whereabouts of any of the four that she had given up.

Elizabeth's questions to the workhouse had gone unanswered, she was simply told, "your children were placed under our guardianship and all parental rights taken from you, as such you have no right to know anything about them at all."

She knew Hilda her eldest daughter, who was now a married 23 year old, was fighting to get the authorities to consider releasing Florence into her care, a fight that was hampered by the fact that she wasn't "next of kin". Hilda however, vowed that she would never give up the quest to help Florence. Pleading and sometimes angry letters were sent by her to Eastry Workhouse, letters begging and later demanding to know why her younger sister was not kept with Lillian and Irene during their circle of homes.

The letters were either ignored or if answered, unhelpful. No longer in the institutions that had been "home" throughout their childhood, Lillian and Irene were now adults with one longing, a longing to find their mother. She had neglected them in favour of her own needs, had survived in the only way she could but she was still their mother and the girls had missed her terribly. Lillian decided that she was going to find their mother. She could remember the area she lived in before being sent to the workhouse and believed that she should try there first.

The walk from Eastry to Woodnesborough was not an unpleasant one, despite the strong wind and the chilly air and Lillian soon reached the local pub. Knowing it wasn't ladylike for a female to enter a pub, she walked slowly past the door, then back again, waiting for some one to either enter or leave the Inn.

"Are you waiting for someone miss?" called a middle aged man as he ambled towards her.

"Sir, I am trying to find my mother," she smiled, "who lived here in Woodnesborough at least until 1913."

"Can't help you then I'm afraid, I've only been here since 1915," he replied.

"You could try asking old Mrs D'Arcy," he continued, "she's lived here most of her life so I've heard. She lives about quarter of a mile away. Stay on this side of the lane, and her cottage is the second one along from here, you can't miss it."

"Thank you so much," called Lillian who was already walking in the direction the kindly man had indicated.

Having passed the little church of St Mary the Virgin, standing aloof on a slight knoll with its odd cupola-capped wooden addition to the balustrade tower, Lillian found herself outside a tiny cottage with its garden of ancient fruit trees and fences wreathed in shrub roses, climbers and ramblers. Lillian suddenly felt very vulnerable. She was unsure now whether to knock on the door or not. Her mind was made up for her when suddenly the door opened and a very large lady with a wrinkled face and the bluest eyes Lillian had ever seen stood frowning at her.

"Well I'll be beggared," she exclaimed after a while, "you'll be one of those Hatcher girls wont you?"

"Yes, I'm Lillian," the young woman replied.

"My goodness me, I often wondered what had become of you and the other little ones," cried Mrs D'Arcy, "what are you doing here?"

"I am looking for my mother," said Lillian softly, "does she still live around here?"

"No my lovely," replied the old lady gently, "the whole family moved away some time ago , to a place called Acrise, out Folkestone way."

"Sorry to have bothered you, but thank you for your help," said Lillian as she slowly started back along the road.

Five weeks later after knocking on many doors in order to find her, the Hatcher siblings were reunited with their mother.

For Lillian and Irene being close to her was part of their childhood dreams. No one had cuddled them when they were children, no one had told them they were loved or took an interest in what they had achieved whilst at school.

Their brother Percival met Elizabeth a few times but too much water had passed under the bridge and he told her so. Although only an employee he felt that the Pettit's, with whom he had a happy and trusting relationship, were his family.

Elizabeth Ann Hatcher nee Mitten

Chapter 30

Acrise , where property was divided among a few, took its name from the manor house, Acrise Place.

1 Blandred Cottage, Acrise, which looked as though it lived in dread of the next high wind, was one of two farm cottages set in the centre of a field, a long and some times muddy walk from the nearest road.

With ill fitting doors and windows the cottage appeared to sag through lack of care over the years. Upstairs there were two bedrooms, at the cracked window in one bedroom hung the remnants of a threadbare grey blanket, which blocked all visual escape to the outdoors. At the bottom of the narrow steep stairs was a door to the scullery where a large stone sink perched precariously on two brick pillars. At the rear of the scullery was a pantry within which were two thick stone shelves, providing an area on which to place milk, meat and lard, any food that needed to be kept cool. As Elizabeth and Richard lived hand to mouth, the stone shelves were more often than not, empty

Opposite the scullery was a living room with a big black open range, there was no floor covering, just rough uneven bricks sank into the earth at odd angles through which worms and slugs would rear their heads before the chicken which roamed freely through the cottage, took a peck at them.

Cupboards either side of the fireplace were used for storing anything from clothes and shoes to old sacks and out of date newspapers. Once a year the newspapers were used for papering over or stuffing into the crumbling walls of the cottage. The sacks cut to size were used for wash cloths, table covers even sanitary towels. All lighting came from candles and the heating for the whole cottage from the logs burned on the range.

In the adjoining field was the well from which water was drawn by bucket. During the summer the well would dry up for a few days, it was then that the bottom of it was cleared of the decayed bodies of mice, moles, rats and frogs as well as old tins and any other object that had been thrown in.

A tin bath lent against an old wooden shed at the side of the cottage. Inside the shed, two buckets and sheets of newspaper cut into squares and threaded with string served as a toilet for the inhabitants of both cottages. When the buckets were filled to brimming with human waste and crawling with flies, a hole would be dug on the edge of the field and the contents of the buckets disposed of.

At the rear of each cottage was a small garden which served as a tiny vegetable plot that provided a little food during the week. Seasonal vegetables not grown in the garden were acquired come nightfall, from the farmer's fields. The half a dozen chickens were fed on household scraps if there were any and the odd handful of corn taken from the farm.

This was where Lillian, having moved in with her mother, stepfather and their three children, now lived a miserable hand to mouth existence along with her youngest brother Eddie.

It was here at Acrise that Lillian met her husband-to-be, Percival Bailey. His parents lived in the adjoining cottage and he was on leave from the Army.

A fresh faced man, 5ft 7ins tall with brown hair and eyes, Percival Charles Bailey had spent the past four years in the

2nd Battalion, The Buffs, having joined in September 1919 at Canterbury, Kent along with his brothers and father. The Buffs had spent time in India, Mesopotamia and lastly in Aden. As a Medical Orderly, Percival had seen young men made old with physical and mental scarring brought about by the horrors of war, the visions of which would stay with him throughout his life. Percy as he was known was de-mobbed in Hounslow in September 1923 and immediately travelled to Kent to his beloved Lillian.

She smiled as soon as she saw him striding across the fields towards Blandred Cottages. Percy's first thought as he held his future wife was of how tired she looked, worry lines already playing around her young brow and he soon learnt why. As well as worrying about the baby she was carrying and the stigma that went with being unmarried, she had been told that when the baby arrived they would have to find somewhere else to live. There was no room for anyone else in such tiny cottages.

Percy's parents lived in much the same way as Lillian's, in a damp cramped cottage. Sticky flypaper which was black with flies and seldom changed hung in the middle of the front room. Chickens roamed through the cottage leaving their droppings wherever they could.

His father was a tall man with a long thick beard who used to repair the family's shoes while sitting in the huge armchair next to the fire with the cobbler's last (an iron shoe form) on his lap.

Percy's mother was a short plump woman who always wore the same long black skirt day after day and whose furrowed brow spoke of the hardships she had encountered. She was also a very superstitious person who would cover the only mirror in the house with any old rag she could find when lightning was about. If anyone broke the mirror, she believed that they would all have seven years bad luck, as if their luck could get any worse. Living with them were three children, Fred was 15 and their natural son. Jack was born in 1916. He never knew how he came to live at Blandred Cottages, he never asked and his foster parents never told him.

The youngest child Stanley was given to the Bailey family along with £5.00 on a railway station, after being advertised in a local paper. His unmarried mother was desperate, the boy's father had left her and she was in danger of losing her job if she kept the child. She had thought of abandoning the child but then changed her mind. If she was caught she would be imprisoned. Advertising him in the paper had obvious advantages to her - it was simple and quick with few questions asked.

These two families managed as best they could with what little they had and when work was scarce and food was in short supply they would often resort to eating hedgehogs. After rolling them in a mixture of mud and clay they were cooked over an open fire. When cooked the hedgehog's skin came off as the mud and clay mixture was removed, leaving the meat which was then served with whatever vegetables were available.

Various family members periodically spent short periods of time in the workhouse especially during the winter months. They were so poor they could not afford to buy a sack of coal. Instead once a month, one of the boys trudged to the nearest coal merchant with a few coppers and bought twenty-eight pounds of it. The merchant wouldn't consider delivering this amount, it being too small. Hoisting the coal on his back the child would stagger home, a clear message to all who saw them that they were the "*poor pauper children*". Many a time they wished they could stop a while to move the sack a bit and stop one particular coal lump from digging into a shoulder or a lower arm. No child dared to stop though; they knew they would be punished if they dawdled. Supplemented with wood from the nearby copse, the coal would provide welcome heat for a short time.

All of these people from the eldest to the very youngest would work in the fields picking or planting potatoes, hoeing and dung spreading. In the school holidays the children would harvest potatoes and so supplement the family income. At night they would go home crying with pain in their bodies after a day's back breaking work.

Percy pleaded with Richard Saxby and his own parents, "Let us stay, we could sleep on the floor. We have no where else."

"Use your common sense lad," said his father, "there just isn't room for you."

"What about the possibility of work with a tied cottage?" Percy enquired of the farmer. "There might be a little work some time in the future but definitely no cottage," replied the farmer, "I have no more cottages."

"The barn then, can we stay in the barn?" begged Percy.

With a deep sigh the farmer replied, "Very well, but only for one night, it really is most unsuitable. You will be using candles I presume and the barn and all the straw will be at risk of fire, not to mention yourselves."

Lillian was totally distraught; she had only just left a life of being shunted from workhouse to training homes. She had seen first hand the heartbreak and devastation that separating husbands, wives and children had bought. Now it seemed that the workhouse was to be her home again when all she wanted was Percy and the baby she was carrying. A family of her own, that loved and laughed, cried and cuddled and shared dreams of the future with each other. The family she had never had.

Chapter 31

Just after 7am the following day, having spent much of the night discussing what to do in order to stay out of the workhouse Lillian and Percy went to plead with the farmer once again and on leaving had permission from him to build their "home".

The farmer walked away, shaking his head, unsure of whether he had done the right thing or not. All he knew for certain was that he hadn't the heart to throw the young couple off his land and told them to help themselves to any old bits and pieces that were lying around the farm and to make sure their home was built out of sight of the track.

All day Percy dug. Deeper and wider he dug until his back, shoulders and arms felt numb. Lillian despite her advanced state of pregnancy lifted heavy buckets of earth and carried them to the edge of the field where, after emptying them she raked the contents flat to blend in with the rest of the ground. Liquid filled blisters the size of her finger nails had formed on her hands, some had burst and flaps of dirt encrusted skin hung from her palms. The baby inside her kicked hard all day long as if in some type of protest. The digging complete, Percy shored up the side with pieces of corrugated tin and at 1am by the dim light of the moon, he threw bales of straw into the hole that he had spent all day digging.

Inside, Lillian dragged the straw to one area and made a mound the size of a small bed. Over this she placed old corn sacks, given to them by the farmer. Four other sacks she saved as covers. On the bare earth opposite the straw bed she stood an old enamel bucket, covered the bottom with some stones to keep it steady and between these they wedged a candle. This was their only means of light and heat. Percy meanwhile, had gone to the well and had drawn water which he poured into an old tin pan. He called Lillian and together they walked to the edge of the field, squatted by the hedge and with icy cold water, washed away their grime and sweat. Teeth chattering, noses running and bodies racked with cold they made their way, hand in hand, back to their "home".

After helping Lillian down the makeshift ladder he had made from the bottom of an old bedstead, Percy followed her and reaching up, pulled lengths of rusting tin over the top of the hole. Their "home" now had a roof. Still in the clothes they had been toiling in all day, they lay on the straw bed, covered themselves with the sacks and wrapped their arms around each other for extra warmth. Although every bone in her body ached and she just wanted to sleep, Lillian found it impossible to do so. She was freezing cold and dampness hung all around her. She opened her eyes as wide as she could in the hope that she would see something, anything. She hated this darkness. Every now and then a slight scurrying sound came from over head, a mouse or stoat going about its early morning business. When the first light of dawn came drifting through the chinks in the tin roof, Lillian finally fell asleep.

The following morning, Percy went looking for work while Lillian slowly made her way to his parent's cottage. Walking through the small crooked door that led into the tiny scullery, she was immediately engulfed in a mixture of smells, stale tobacco smoke, cat's pee, chicken droppings and dampness plus all the other smells of poverty.

She sat sobbing her heart out to Percy's mother, "I don't know how I am going to cope living in that hole in the ground, it's damp, cold and dirty down there. We are so cold every hour of the day and night. Percy has gone looking for work without even a hot drink inside him and there is no means of cooking him a meal when he returns in the evening."

After the young pregnant girl had calmed down the older woman said, "Lillian, if you buy your own food and help clean up the whole house with me, you can have the use of the grate to cook for you and Percy. I can do nothing else to help you."

Thus the routine began, Lillian would go and help clean the cottage, in return she was able to cook Percy a hot dinner. Most days this consisted of potatoes and a few vegetables. At other times a vegetable hotpot with a piece of not too fresh bread, the crust of which was ripped off and saved ready to be dunked in the cup of tea that followed.

Lillian Agnes Hatcher was married on 23rd October 1923 to Percival Charles Bailey at Elham, Kent. Eight months pregnant she wore her one piece of decent clothing a calf length, loose straight shift dress that covered her swollen belly. As well as being Lillian's birth month, October was one of her favourite months of the year. She loved the beautiful colours of the leaves just before they fell from the trees, stunning colours of gold and red, orange and yellow.

Marriage altered nothing for Lillian and Percy, they still had to call a hole in the ground their home. Worse still, they would have to bring a new life into this so called home.

November heralded the start of winter, the trees were bare and underfoot the soft crunch heralding the first signs of frost could be heard. As the snow flurries began, their home became damper and colder despite extra bales of straw now lining the inner walls. They managed to borrow a glazed stone hot water bottle from another farm worker but had to rely on someone in the cottages having the grate alight so they could get hot water.

Lillian's half sister, Hilda, whose husband had a reasonably well paid job, visited Blandred Cottages one Sunday in December of that year riding pillion on her husbands Triumph motorbike. Unable to drive right down to the cottages, her husband sat at the edge of the dirt track and waited for his wife to return. Hilda had bought gifts of food to help her mother whose entire household was now on Parish Relief. Two loaves of bread, a lump of mutton, a pudding basin filled with dripping, some tea, a slab of cake and some margarine were all neatly tucked into Hilda's wicker basket.

Walking towards the little cottages, shooing the hens from her feet at the same time trying to side-step layers of excreta they had left behind she suddenly saw what she thought was a very pregnant Lillian heaving herself out of a large hole in the ground. Hilda stood open mouthed as her younger sister made her way to where she was standing, she couldn't believe Lillian had been reduced to living the way she was. Grabbing her by the hand and at the same time taking in the deep shadows under her sister's eyes, Hilda pulled her into their mother's cottage.

Banging the wicker basket on the table she forcibly removed one of the children from the hard backed chair in front of the window.

"Sit there Lillian and don't move till I get back," she shouted before striding, red in the face, back to her husband.

"Frank," she ordered, "take me back home and then return for Lillian. She is living in a bloody hole in the ground, and I'll tell you this, no sister of mine is going to give birth in a place like that."

By evening Lillian having had a long hot bath was warm and snug in the smallest bedroom of Hilda's house. Percy, who had been given the opportunity of work on the farm the following day, stayed at the "home" they had made in Acrise.

Hilda's kindness came at just the right time, by the following morning five inches of snow covered some parts of

Southern England. A hole in the ground was no place for a child to be born at any time least of all in the cold of winter. Once the snow had melted, the two sisters walked the short distance from Hilda's house to the main street of Dover, its famous white cliffs looking out to sea, a symbol of England seen by travellers whether departing for or arriving from the continent just 21 miles away. They walked down the street chatting about the things sisters do, including the 1905 extended tramway that ran from Dover to Crabble and River for only a penny, Lillian's lack of a home, the birth of her baby, and how to help their sister. "How many years had passed since they had last seen Florence? Was her life any worse than Lillian's? Did she still remember them?" They both had so many questions but still no answers.

They stopped now and then to gaze in the shop windows which were bursting with all manner of different gift ideas, tempting those with money to step inside and buy.

By mid-afternoon the sisters had finished their Christmas shopping which included lace trimmed handkerchiefs for Florence which Hilda hoped would be forward to her via the Workhouse and a small gift for each of Hilda's two children. Making their way back home they met the rag and bone man, an odd looking little man who always wore a cap and a scruffy muffler round his neck and stood at the end of Herbert Street with his two wheeled wooden hand cart calling out for "any old rags or woollies."

"Have you any baby clothes among those rags?" Hilda enquired.

"I'm collecting rags, not selling them lady," came the glib reply.

"I'm well aware of that," Hilda retorted, "so don't try and get smart with me! I can pay you as much as the rag picker you work for does, so what's the problem? It's a bit extra in your pocket. And don't forget I'm one of your regulars; you've had plenty of rags off of me over the years. Anyway, I want the best of any baby clothes you have."

He muttered under his breath, "I'm not being spoken to like that by a woman." while at the same time picking tiny clothes out of the assortment of rags that formed a mound in the centre of his cart. After much puffing and panting embroidered with the odd curse, he found several well used items, placed them in some equally well used newspaper and took the thruppence offered by Hilda.

He thought the items were worth more but the hard fixed stare on the older woman's face told him it would be useless to ask.

"She's right," he thought. "Thruppence is better than nothing and probably more than I would have received from the rag picker".

Touching his cap and bidding the two women a good afternoon he was on his way again, the noise of his hobnailed boots and the iron rimmed wheels resounding on the cobbled stones.

Percy arrived for the weekend on Saturday evening, December 20th and after taking off his snow clogged shoes and wiping away the dewdrop that was hanging from his nose he held his hands, blue with the cold in front of the fire. Lillian, Hilda and her husband sat at the table drinking tea and gossiping whilst eating a thick slice of bread pudding and Percy gladly joined them with both the gossiping and the eating.

The labour pains that had started that afternoon as nothing more than a dull ache were now becoming intense.

"I feel like going for a slow walk, just to the end of the street," said Lillian.

Percy pushed his chair away from the table, "I'll walk with you," he said, "just give me time to get your coat and hat. It's bitter out there."

As Lillian stood up, water poured down her legs and she

knew that their baby was on its way. There was no pain relief available for home births and with each contraction Lillian thought she was going to pass out.

Hilda delivered her nephew, Ronald Charles Stephen Bailey in the early hours of Sunday 21st December. Having removed the newspaper, which held the remains of the after-birth from under her sister's bottom, Hilda washed the newborn child and handed him to Lillian, at the same time shouting to Percy, to make everyone a cup of strong tea. Lillian, her face drenched with sweat and her lips dry and cracked, gazed at her perfect son with his rich dark brown hair, olive skin and hazel eyes. At last she had a family and cradling her son as he lay peacefully in her arms she wondered how her own mother could have ever parted with her own children.

Hilda walked into Dover town the following day and registered the birth of the baby. She lied when the registrar asked for the permanent address of the newborn, telling him that her address was the permanent abode of her sister and the baby. How could she ever begin to explain that Lillian's home was a hole in the ground and that the baby would be living there too? Ronald would be taken away by the authorities and Hilda knew her sister had already suffered enough.

Security was the only thing missing from Lillian's life now. If only they could all stay here at her sister's home, but she knew that could never be. A small rented terrace house, it was home to Hilda and her husband, two young children and her elderly mother-in-law. At the start of the New Year the young couple and their baby would have to return to Acrise.

On the 5th January 1924 with the Christmas festivities just a memory, Lillian woke with a feeling of dread, this was the day she would return to her own "home". The few items they had acquired since being in Dover were being loaded onto a cart by Percy and Frank.

"Here, take this," ordered Hilda holding up a small chair with one leg slightly shorter than the others, "It'll be far more comfortable than straw to sit on whilst feeding the baby."

There was also an old pram which had been used by his children, that Frank had secretly cleaned, repaired and repainted. Lillian squealed with delight when she saw it, she was so grateful, now her baby would not have to sleep on the straw bed, which would be permanently damp by the moisture of the earth beneath it.

For their night-time ablutions Hilda gave them an old rusty bucket

"You don't," Hilda informed them, "want to be going across to the hedge at night, use the bucket and empty it in the morning"

A well-used saucepan, a small kettle, a box of candles, some odd cutlery and a couple of chipped dishes and cups were placed into one of two cotton flour sacks. There were also two bars of soap and a second-hand Primus stove complete with a tin of paraffin. The second sack contained a couple of serviceable blankets, two cushions to use as a mattress in the baby's pram, some small towels and the few clothes Lillian had bought since living at Dover.

"If you look after the sacks," Hilda said, "when you eventually find yourselves a house can unpick the seams, wash them several times which will remove the printing and turn them a lovely cream colour. They can then be made into curtains."

In her wicker shopping basket, Hilda put four loaves of what she called stale bread although it was only two days old and was quite fresh inside.

"The hard crust," she told them, "is good for your teeth."

The basket also held some meat cubes, a small amount of tea and some milk that she had put in an old lemonade bottle which closed by way of an iron stopper and rubber washer.

"Thank you both so very much," said Lillian as she kissed her sister and hugged Frank.

"You're more than welcome," replied Hilda.

Cradling the sleeping baby in the crook of her arm, Lillian climbed onto the cart after which Percy picked up the reins and firmly but gently flicked the cart-horse across its back. At the end of the sloping cobbled track that led down to the main street, Lillian looked back and with tears in her eyes waved to the couple who had been so kind to her and her husband.

At Acrise the baby was laid on the bed of straw while the pram and other items were unloaded from the cart.

Percy knew he would have to make the hole bigger as the pram took up so much room and he didn't want to stand the primus or candles too close to his newborn son. By 7pm, the baby was sleeping soundly. Two candles burning in the bucket gave a dim flickering orange light and on the primus stove, steam from a kettle of water nearly at the boil. Lillian crumbled two meat cubes into dishes along with two chunks of bread from one of the loaves; over this she poured the hot water. Sitting on the straw bed they ate their evening meal as the cold night air forced its way into their "home" through every available crevice.

An hour later Percy pinched the candles out with the tips of his moistened thumb and forefinger and lay down next to his wife. Soon they were both asleep.

Two days later Percy came in from the farm, beaming from ear to ear.

"Guess what girl," he said, slapping Lillian's bottom playfully, "I've been offered permanent, part time employment on the farm with the opportunity of full time employment later in the year. There's still no accommodation and the wage is very low but it's better than nothing. Now I've got regular work, we can look for rented accommodation. Life is going to get better now, I know it is."

Chapter 32

Lillian first noticed the baby was unwell at the end of February 1924. He appeared to be losing weight, cried a lot and was very restless.

Two hours after taking his feed Ronald vomited, soaking the well scrubbed sack that was his sheet with green bile. His little face turned crimson as he let out long pitiful howls of pain whilst bringing his once chubby knees up to his tummy. An hour later he was asleep, his breathing interrupted every so often with a deep sob. Later that evening when the only meal of the day was finished, Lillian filled the old stone hot water bottle and laid it at the end of Ronald's pram hoping that her baby would get some comfort from the heat. She listened to the freely offered theories and advice given to her by both her mother and mother-in-law.

"Well, he's a couple of months old now," her mother-in-law said, "perhaps he's hungry and need's a little more food. Try a tiny piece of bread, soaked in a mixture of milk and water that might help him".

"You're just a nervous mother, you should relax," her mother sniffed "It's nothing but a fever or a chill, babies get chills, cover him up and let him sweat it out. If it's not that then it could be that your milk is no good for him, perhaps he needs cow's milk."

Her mother's intuition told Lillian it was none of these things and putting Ronald in his pram, she pushed him the four miles to Dr Waite's house. On the return journey, with the tiny green bottle of medicine prescribed for Ronald safely tucked under the top cover of the pram Lillian asked God to forgive the lies she had just told the Doctor. She had lied about where she was living telling the Doctor that she now lived with her mother at Blandred Cottages. She had lied about the amount she had to eat, saying that they all had three meals a day. She was too ashamed to tell the truth, to say they were living in a hole in the ground, that she couldn't remember the last time she had eaten even one good meal in a day.

March 1924 and the lambing season was under way. Percy and one of the other farm labourers had just started the task of counting the number of lambs born overnight when a cry from Lillian, full of grief and anguish filled the early morning air.

She had known as soon as she went to Ronald's pram that he had gone, his little body no longer able to cope with the constant diarrhoea or the sickness. His tiny face just visible above the bedding looked like porcelain, long eyelashes curled onto his baby cheeks. For what seemed an eternity, Lillian felt that she couldn't breathe, could feel her heart pounding into her chest while her head felt as though it was floating above her. Her legs suddenly buckled beneath her and she sank to the floor of the hole that was her home.

Ronald was two and a half months old when he died of gastroenteritis. Percy and Lillian buried their baby, covered with a blanket that would never warm his body again, in a corner of a little churchyard not far from Blandred Cottages. The burial over, all the couple were left with were the "what ifs" and "should haves".

Lillian began packing the few items that her first born had into the pram, his little baby clothes, a tiny rattle that was his first and only Christmas present from her and Percy. The well washed sacks that were his blankets. Into her bag carefully wrapped in paper, she placed the tiny curl that Percy had cut from their son's head before his funeral, at the same time crying for her dead baby and cursing the way they had to live. Her greatest wish was that someone would help them to find somewhere decent to live, however small or in need of repair. Thoughts of a decent house filled her head. A house that was warm and cosy, somewhere she could call home. She imagined how neat and pretty it would look with fresh clean curtains at every window, a table covered with a deep red cloth. Logs piled high by the fireplace and the larder filled with food. Coming back to reality, she continued to pack away the rest of her son's meagre belongings.

Five months later she heard John Wheatley the Minister of Health planned to build 190,000 new council houses at modest rents in 1925 and that by 1934 that figure would increase to 450,000. The government stated that, "it was essential that each house should contain a living room, parlour and scullery, larder and bathroom with three bedrooms upstairs, two of which must be capable of containing two beds."

Although not particularly religious, Lillian had always said her favourite prayer each night,

"Lord I am not worthy for you to come to me,
But see how much I need you Lord and come and live in me,
And may your body guide me Lord, through all harm and ill,
And when your life is in me Lord, help me to do Thy will".

Now though, she asked for a little more from her Lord, she asked that she and Percy would be among some of the first people to be housed.

For some time afterwards Lillian would imagine that she could hear her Lord's voice answering her, telling her that he had heard her prayers and soon everything would be alright, they would have a lovely home one day.

She didn't know it then, but it would be the 1940s before she and Percy would be given a council house. For them the hole in the ground was their home for some time despite many attempts to better themselves.

Chapter 33

Folkestone, the nearest town to Blandred Cottages had returned to its role as a holiday resort after WW1. However this time it was a holiday destination for families not as the resort of the gentry as it had been before. Large older type homes were turned into flats as housing developments took place in the town as a way to meet housing shortages. Amusement centres were established along the sea front and a zigzag path on the West Cliff was built.

It was here in Folkestone that Percy spent long, tiring evenings knocking on doors asking for employment, explaining that he would do any job however menial as long as the wage was such that he could leave the farm and so get decent accommodation. He would do anything to get away from the hell he was in.

On his day off he would call at every building site and ask to speak to the foreman, plead for a job of any kind even if it was sweeping the rubble from where the skilled men were working, he would carry planks of wood or stack bricks. After three weeks, he gave up. It seemed to Percy that everyone in Folkestone was looking for work. There were too many people, chasing too few jobs. He would never find work in the town.

By November 1924 Percy had been "promoted" to other work on the farm, though there was very little increase in the wage he received. He had always been an adaptable person and became quite a handy man, at times being a tractor driver or a shepherd as well as learning to shear and dip the sheep. In fact he had done almost every farm job including potato picking, singling the cattle beet and stone picking.

No matter how hard he worked though, there was still no accommodation for him and Lillian. Percy knew that he must find another job with a tied cottage, living life as they were was becoming more difficult for the young couple each day. Lillian spent most of her time crying, she was pregnant again, pregnant and frightened. No child would ever survive such appalling conditions she knew that from bitter experience.

When Percy returned from the fields at night he and Lillian would usually have words over who was to blame for the predicament they were in. Angry heated words that altered nothing. Only they could do that. Every Sunday he would walk miles to different farms asking for work with any type of accommodation while Lillian made sure that upon his return there would be something hot for him to eat and for a while, they would forget about the angry words.

Christmas was looming again and as with other Christmas's the residents at Blandred Cottages had nothing. Once again Hilda came to the rescue with a large basket of food. Percy vowed that one day, somehow, he would repay her for her kindness.

That opportunity came just after the lambing had finished in 1925. One of the ewe's had managed to get out of the field and was lazily chewing the lush grass that was growing by the edge of the little dirt track that ran from the fields to the cottages. Its lamb lay sleeping a few feet away. Slowly and quietly Percy walked over to the ewe, grabbed hold of her thick woolly coat and pulling her head back, cut her throat.

Making sure she was quite dead, he hoisted the blood soaked animal over his shoulders and staggering under the weight, made his way home. Once the farmhouse was in sight he pushed the sheep's body as far as he could under the hedge, just in case the farmer was around. He was taking a huge risk and prayed he wouldn't get caught.

Lillian screamed as her husband, smothered in blood from his hair to the back of his knees, lowered him-self into their home. He explained what he had done and asked his wife to get him a couple of old sacks. In one he cut two holes for his arms and another for his head. Taking off his blood soaked clothes he slipped the sack over his head. Darkness had started to fall as Percy crept back to the ewe's body, placed it on the other sack and dragged it the few hundred yards to his parent's house.

In the scullery, working by the light of candles Percy and his father set about dissecting the animal. After stripping the skin from the back legs, they broke the legs off below the back knees, tied rope to them and hoisted the body up over the door ramming a stick between the leg bones to keep the legs apart. Carefully, they began stripping off the skin. A strong arm was needed to punch and pull the skin off, and Percy being the youngest and strongest was nominated for the job. Once the skin was completely removed the sternum was opened. They pulled out the intestines carefully so as not to rupture them and spill the contents of food and manure over the scullery floor. Once the intestines were removed and put into a bucket they were covered with the fleece, ready to be removed to the hole being dug by Percy's brother.

Later, Hilda was proudly given the best mutton chops in payment for her kindness to Percy and Lillian. Everyone lived very well for a while on the meat from the ewe, nothing was wasted even the head was used to make two pots of broth. When the last of it was eaten Percy went back to his usual means of acquiring meat for the pot. He went poaching.

With some old copper wire in his pocket he would walk to the local wood with his father's two ferrets in a sack where they wriggled and fought trying to make their escape. Once he was deep in the wood he made his snares using the wire and set them over a few rabbit holes, sent the ferrets down and sat and waited for the rabbits to be chased up. After he had legged the rabbits (cutting a hole in one leg and passing the other leg through it) he squeezed the urine from the bladder so as the meat didn't become tainted. Swinging the dead rabbits by their back legs, he then began the walk home happy in the knowledge that there would be some meat on the table for a day or two. The skins he saved for the rag and bone man, who would examine them to see if they were in good shape and after much light hearted banter would buy them from Percy for a couple of coppers.

A daughter Molly Irene was born to Percy and Lillian on the 14th May 1925, a gorgeous little girl with brown hair, blue eyes and little pink cheeks. Molly was born in one of the cottages. Her grandmother, fearful of another baby dying, allowed her son and his family to stay with her. The cottage was depressingly overcrowded, another son and his family were also living there. Sharing one bedroom were three underfed, runny nosed children and their parents, the parents in the double bed, the children beside it. In the other bedroom slept Percy's parents and his brothers.

Percy, Lillian and their baby slept downstairs in the parlour, Molly in the old armchair and her parents on a layer of sacks in front of the chair so that should the baby roll off the chair in the night, she would fall on one of them and not on the brick floor.

Mornings were horrendous, so many individuals all with different needs trying to go about their business in a two bed roomed cottage. The men washed and shaved in cold water, drank a couple of mugs of tea and then left the cottage to look for or go to work.

Once the men had gone, the women would take the few rags that passed as bed-clothes and put them across the foot of the bed and aired them for a few hours before throwing back on the bed again.

The rugs were then taken outside where the women hung them over the wash line and beat them with large sticks removing the dirt, dust and chicken muck whilst the older children took turns to go to the well to fetch water for the day.

Once the three older children's morning chores were completed, they would start the long walk across the fields to school. In the summer the walk didn't take too long but on winter's days it took nearly twice the time to reach the warmth of the classroom.

It was here that the children wrapped near frozen hands round the big iron water pipes that ran round the classroom. A back boiler behind an open fire heated the water in the pipes. When the weather was wet the pipes would be draped with a variety of children's clothing and before long a steady cloud of steam would be floating to the rafters. There was an array of socks, mittens and shoes. Sturdy weatherproof boots of those who were fortunate enough to own them stood on the floor under the pipes. When it rained or snowed the children's shoes, complete with gaping holes in the soles were always on top of the pipes.

A pail of hot cocoa was provided for the children on extremely cold days, half a tin cup each gulped down eagerly after which it was down to the business of learning, before the long wet trudge home in the afternoon.

Sunday was a day of prayer for the children who went to Sunday school every Sabbath. Prayers over, they would walk back home across the fields arriving just in time for dinner. After dinner, with hands and faces washed and hair brushed it was back to Church again to sing in the choir.

Sunday was also bath night for the children. The eldest child was first, bathed and dried with a towel that had to do for the whole family. They all used the same water in the tin bath which was "topped up" if they were lucky, before the next child bathed. Sometimes they would bathe in front of a nice blazing fire. When coal was in short supply though, their bath would be in front of dying embers in near cold water. The bath was then emptied by scooping the now filthy water out with a bucket.

Clean underwear for the week was put on before they made their way up to bed, sometimes with a full belly, other times crying with hunger. Not that crying did the child any good as this was met with a swift, hard clip 'round the ear.

Every Monday morning the wash day routine began at Blandred Cottages just after 6am. While the main laundry was being washed in the tin bath, the clothes worn all week were put into of pails of water and left to soak. An overpowering stench of a week's body sweat, stale tobacco and the smells of the farmyard filled the tiny cottages as soon as the garments touched the water. When the weather was bad the sculleries in both cottages were festooned with wet clothes suspended from lengths of string that crisscrossed the ceilings. The clothes took so long to dry indoors that at times they hung there so long they started to grow mould. At other times they were just worn damp.

Chapter 34

Another crisis hit the Bailey family in 1926 when Percy's elder bother suddenly left his wife and their two children. However hard he tried he was unable to forget the horrors of war. Exploding mines, the sight and sounds of his comrades ripped to pieces by flying shrapnel, the screams of young boys and men buried alive while hiding in their dugouts. All of these things implanted on his mind during the day and invading his dreams at night and turning them into nightmares. No matter where he was or what he was doing, when the sights and sounds started playing in his head, he would bang his head on anything that was near him, a wall, a table or a door. The usual conditions associated with prolonged loss of sleep then rapidly took over, irritability, emotional instability and the inability to concentrate. Nothing the doctor gave him helped.

One morning after a meagre breakfast, washed down with tea that had been reheated from the evening before, he had gone to work with Percy. As the brothers neared the farmyard his brother informed Percy that he was never going back to work on the farm nor was he going home to his wife and children.

"You don't mean that surely," exclaimed Percy, "what will your wife and children do without you, how will they ever manage?"

"I really don't know, but they will have to manage because I mean it, I am never going home or back to work."

"Look, why don't you talk to me about what is happening to you," pleaded Percy, "you know the old saying, a trouble shared is a trouble halved."

Despite Percy's desperate pleas for him to talk to him, his brother just carried on walking.

It was left to Percy to explain to his sister-in-law who didn't believe a word of what she had heard. She knew her husband was prone to fits of depression but couldn't believe he would leave her and his children. Leave the whole family destitute.

Several local people reported various encounters with Percy's brother in the following month and many tried to persuade him to return home. He would just mutter about the war and how he was going to save his mates. He would lay on his belly, twigs and leaves stuck into his hair as camouflage in his "lookout" under a ditch. Every morning for the next two weeks Percy would take whatever food he could spare to his brother and try to persuade him to return home. One morning his brother had gone. He was seen roaming about four miles away a few days later and then he just disappeared.

Three months later his distraught wife left the children, both girls, with their grandfather and grandmother Bailey saying she could no longer feed and clothe them and as it was their son that had left her they could now take on his responsibilities and look after the children. The girls watched their mother walk across the fields and out of sight, unaware that she would never be coming back for them.

Two sacks of straw were placed at the foot of the bed in a room already overcrowded. In a family already close to starving, two more mouths to feed.

Church elders arranged for a collection of old clothes and a small amount of food to be given to the Bailey family. For a while there were full bellies and clothes for everyone. It didn't matter that the clothes were either too big or too small and the children hated them, they had to wear them.

Jumpers with the sleeves shortened, the edges left to fray. Skirts that were meant for adults, held up with a pin at the waist and the hem cut none to straight, to the correct length. At school they were ridiculed, laughed at and called names. Most afternoons the Bailey children would walk home in tears. Only once did they tell their grandparents of their daily ordeal and how they hated the clothes. The answer was "stick up for yourselves and as for the clothes, it's them or nothing"

Before long the girls became too much for the ageing grandparents to cope with. If the house was larger and they had a decent income things would have been so different. Their grandfather was still rising early in the morning and working on the farm till sunset for paltry wages that barely covered keeping two people. There was never enough food and as the girls grew, so did their appetites, the grandparents knew they would have to provide for the girls for some years.

The following year after many discussions within the family, an advert was placed in a paper asking for anyone willing to take the two children. Three weeks later the girls, washed and dressed in the better of their clothes and their hair brushed to a shine, sat gazing through the tiny window that overlooked the dirt track leading to the cottage. Today was the day. A lady, "a posh lady" their grandmother had said, was coming to take them to live in a big house. They would have pretty clothes that fitted them nicely, proper shoes without holes and lots of nice food.

Suddenly a car was in sight, making its way across the bumpy track leaving a trail of dust in its wake. Slowly the car came to a halt and the chauffeur whilst bowing slightly, helped a richly dressed woman alight from one of the rear doors. With a wave of her hand, the chauffeur immediately returned to his place in the driving seat while the woman walked briskly to the cottage door. She was a tall upright woman with thin over plucked eyebrows and an ample bosom, under which she placed her equally ample arms as she spoke.

An amount of money was given to the girls' grandfather and with a curt nod, the woman left taking the two children with her. They were on their way to a new life. The car faded into the distance with two little hands waving from the back window. The waving stopped. The Bailey family never heard of them again.

Chapter 35

Percy and Lillian were now living permanently with Percy's parents - not an ideal situation but better than the hole in the ground and Percy's parents welcomed the half rent paid by their son. The arrangement worked well. Lillian did most of the housework and worked part time in the farmhouse whilst her ageing mother-in-law kept a watchful eye on Molly.

Over the next four years Lillian and Percy had two more children who they named David and Joan. Once again the tiny cottage was overcrowded and with overcrowding came the squalor and the rows. Most mornings a row would erupt between the adults. Petty rows about who had not cleaned the grate, who was wearing someone else's shirt or who hadn't washed yesterday's dishes.

Molly by this time had grown into a rather shy, reserved five year old who had been attending school for nearly a year where often she would leave the house to walk to school with the sounds of the adults raised angry voices ringing in her ears.

She looked upon school, with its windows so high that none of the pupils could look out of them, not only as place of learning but also a quiet haven and liked being there despite its strict regime. Once morning assembly was over, the order from the school teacher was always the same, "Sit down, sit still, be quiet and speak when your spoken to, raise your right hand if you wish to speak and you will call me SIR when you speak to me, you will stand up when I come into the room and remain standing until I say sit, understand?"

In unison the pupils replied "Yes SIR."

What Molly disliked was the walk to school. As she crossed the fields she would always think of what was ahead. The dark foreboding wood was her nightmare. How she hated that part of her journey. The fallen leaves and twigs crunched under foot making her jump. When the wind was high, the bent, twisted and gnarled arms of the huge trees would sway towards her, as if to block her way. Despite the dread of what may be around her Molly would stand and listen, just in case she wasn't alone. All she ever heard was the sound of her own breath, the pounding in her ears and the rustling noises of tiny woodland animals scurrying to their hiding places.

At times Molly became so frightened she would cry, it was then that the trees seemed to look down and whisper to her, shh shh, as the wind blew through the leaves. How pleased she was when two years later her brother David started at the school. He wasn't frightened of walking through the woods. It gave him the opportunity of looking for bird's nests on the way home. Boys loved collecting bird's eggs and David was no exception. He was quite clever at finding the nests and soon came to recognised most of the eggs. If the tree was very tall and two hands were needed for the descent he would pop the birds eggs into his mouth, placing one each side. Once back on the ground he would take the pin that was holding his trousers up and make a hole in each end of the eggs and blow the contents out.

Back at home the eggs were laid in an empty blue sugar bag with layers of grass for protection and then carefully placed in an old cardboard box with his only toy, a tinplate lorry. The lorry's radiator grill was missing but David didn't mind as all of the other parts including the tyres and doors were in working order.

Chapter 36

The farmer explained that it was only a tiny cottage with very steep stairs, the front door didn't quite meet the door frame in places and panes were missing in two windows. Percy had been offered a job on another farm and the cottage was his at a nominal rent. Lillian and Percy were overjoyed, they could not believe they were about to have a home of their own. The next day, Percy gave notice to quit his job and the following Sunday he, Lillian and their three children left Blandred Cottages for good.

Lillian, a maternal and domesticated young woman, worked hard in her first real home and spent the first day washing the walls, floors and windows.

After school was over for the day Molly had charge of her two siblings so that her mother could continue with the cleaning of the cottage. In order to help their mother, the children spent time picking up twigs and larger pieces of wood for the fire, giving them a chance to explore some of the surrounding area.

Percy meanwhile was making the stairs safer. The farmer had warned him that the stairs were very steep but hadn't told him that the banister was missing. A week later, using a length of sturdy rope and large hooks securely embedded in the wall, they had a banister.

Furniture was practically nil but after a few days shelves appeared on the walls in the tiny scullery. These were home to the few saucepans, plates and cups that the couple possessed. A well-washed sack was cut open and threaded at the top with a piece of string. This was attached to hooks on the wall at the side of the stone sink thus hiding from view the area underneath. It was here that Lillian kept her cleaning rags, carbolic soap and scrubbing brushes.

The water butt, which was lying on its side in the garden and was home to several frogs, was thoroughly cleaned and returned to its rightful place by the front door. On the wall next to the water butt, Percy hung the old tin bath.

Their new home, Stone Cottage with its low ceilings and crooked doorframes, was looking better by the day. Lillian was happier than she had been for years. If only her sister Florence could share her happiness.

The following week Lillian was scrubbing the wooden stairs whilst cursing the fact that she felt so ill. She was halfway down having started at the top, when a feeling of nausea washed over her. She looked at the clock; it was just after 9am, too early really to have another mug of tea. Nevertheless she felt so awful she stopped what she was doing and went through to the scullery and poured herself a cup of the strong brew. She instinctively knew what was wrong with her.

Over the next few months, the baby clothes that had been worn by the three older children and packed away "just in case they were needed again" were unpacked and rewashed.

Barbara Elizabeth Ann was born on 23rd July 1934 a tiny girl who was loved by everyone, none more than Molly though, who thought her baby sister was just adorable.

Before long Molly was looking after all of her younger siblings when not at school. She supervised them in the garden, walking through the fields picking cowslips or skipping along the country lane, looking for hedges that boasted thorny bushes full of wild blackberries. The children would spend hours picking the wild black-blue fruit, then with the precious berries lying at the bottom of Barbara's pram, the children would rush home so that their mother could make a blackberry pie - a real treat and how they enjoyed it! What a change it was from the usual meal of bread and margarine or jam or when there was nothing else, bread and lard with a sprinkle of salt.

Sometimes Molly would take her siblings and wander down to the nearest village. There they would sit and watch the blacksmith at work, shoeing the farm carthorses while the smell of burning hooves wafted all around them. If the weather was cold the blacksmith would let them sit near the warm glow of the fire before they made their way back home again.

To help with money, Lillian worked in the fields in the summer, picking fruit or potatoes. In the school holidays the older children, would help out on the farm, loading the sheaves of straw onto the old farm wagon. At midday everyone would stop for a bite to eat and a mug of tea, tea which was hot when it was put into the bottle in the morning but cold by the time it was drunk. Although the children only earned a couple of pence a week they loved being outside and working. At the end of the day they were allowed to watch the huge carthorses drink water from large buckets and afterwards walk with the horses to the stables. The children didn't realise it then but it would not be long before the magnificent horses would be replaced by tractors.

In the latter part of the nineteenth century farm tractors first appeared in a very basic form, but these early types were too unreliable, inefficient and expensive for most farmers to have confidence in. However, by the 1930s, cheaper manufacturing coupled with design improvements resulted in a Ferguson tractor being bought by the owner of the farm. Before long the plowing, tilling, harrowing and planting were done with the tractor and the sight of the carthorses were just a dim memory in the children's minds.

When the farmer had no work for them the Bailey children would sit in the barn and play with the two energetic dogs that prowled the farmyard or watch quietly as the mice scampered between the straw.

Barbara, no longer a baby, had grown into a feisty child with an independent and often rebellious streak but who loved nothing more than listening to her mother bustling around the kitchen singing an old hymn in her gentle voice. Lillian loved all of her children but had already decided there would be no more additions to the family, so she bundled Barbara's outgrown baby clothes into the pram and sold it all to a second-hand shop in Folkestone. With the proceeds of the sale another bed was bought for the children's room. The bed, old and rickety, took up what little space there was but David was very pleased - he had been asking for weeks whether he could have his own bed, stating that he hated sleeping in the same bed as his sisters.

Although life was still hard for Percy and Lillian and they had very few material possessions, they had beautiful children and a house that they were proud to call home. Into this home, despite Lillian declaring that there would be no more children, came two young brothers, William and John. Their own mother was incapable of caring for them so Lillian, with the memories of her own troubled, confused childhood still fresh in her mind, discussed the brothers with Percy. Three weeks later the couple welcomed the boys into their home and their hearts.

The years passed and the stubbornness in them both, led to some very heated rows after which Lillian would leave Percy and stay with her sister. The rows were usually about money or the lack of it and Percy's reluctance to give up his weekly visit to the local pub where he had just one drink. Although he was working all hours of the day the wage Percy received as an agricultural labourer was still very low.

"The grim truth is," he shouted at Lillian, "there are hundreds of people out of work and probably just as many living on handouts from the government after undergoing the means test. At least we don't have the embarrassment of living on assistance. Think yourself damn lucky woman I give you what I can."

It was on one of these occasions after yet another row that Molly was left with her father, the other children having left with Lillian. Percy was fuming, it was a Friday night and he always went for a pint with the other farm labourers on a Friday night. Tonight was going to be no different. He took Molly to a house next to the local pub where a middle-aged woman wearing bright red lipstick and who was "over-fond of the men" greeted him with a peck on the cheek.

Percy explained, "I want a quick pint next door, can Molly stay for an hour?"

"What's up then duck, has Lillian up and left you again?" she cackled, blowing cigarette smoke into Percy's face.

"Not your business is it; all I want to know is can Molly stay a while?" Percy responded.

"Don't get so angry, I was only asking," came the reply, "and of course the girl can stay, she'll be no problem."

Molly was put to bed in a strange room in a stranger's house. The night sky was as black as tar and the child was frightened. She heard the front door close and lay listening for footsteps from the woman downstairs. She heard nothing. Lifting her head just a little she called the woman's name. No one answered. Molly knew then that the woman also had gone to the pub leaving her alone in the house. Pulling the bedclothes which smelt of tobacco smoke, up over her head she laid very still but very alert. She heard every little scurry as a mouse or two ran across the bare floorboards. The window frames rattled as the autumn breeze made its way through into the room.

Several hours later she heard her father's laugh as he, the woman and several of the locals all crowded into the parlour. He opened the bedroom door and called to Molly. When she didn't answer he went to the bed and lifted her into his arms, and took her downstairs whilst telling her what a good girl she had been and they would be going home soon. The woman and her visitors were sitting at the table drinking home made wine when father and daughter entered the room.

All thoughts of leaving for home were gone now as Percy sat watching the pub locals playing games with his daughter. The child didn't understand the rules but laughed at the adults as they played shove ha'penny, all of them trying to shove the coins up the board aiming to get them to fall between the horizontal lines. The areas between each pair of horizontal lines were called "beds" and they were all trying to push the coins so that they landed squarely in the beds without touching the lines. Percy won after getting a coin in each bed three times no easy task but his winnings, the money on the board, was more than welcome and rapidly disappeared into his pocket.

Having become bored with the game, some one suggested that if Molly sang to them they would give her a whole sixpence. The child had never had sixpence for herself before and sixpence was a lot of money. So, after being lifted on to the table so everyone could see her Molly took a deep breath and sung her heart out.

When Molly had finished singing everyone clapped and whistled, while Percy stood grinning like a Cheshire cat.

Lillian returned home after a few weeks as she always did and life continued in its usual way.

Twice a year when the children were on holiday from school and weather, time and money permitted, Lillian would make up little picnic bags of food for them. Then, dressed in the best of their shabby clothes they would walk two miles to the main road to catch a bus into Folkestone where her sister

Hilda would meet them at the bus terminal and together they would walk to the Warren, a natural beauty spot with cliff top walks and access to the beach.

While the two sisters sat and discussed what next should be done in order to obtain news of Florence's release, the children went "exploring". It was quite an adventure for them and they thought they were very brave, negotiating the slippery chalk path down the cliff. All around them they could see lime coloured lichen growing on the stems of the bushes or the jet black coloured berries of the dogwood. Further down the cliff they discovered Sea Kale, its soft green leaves accentuated by its pinky lilac stems.

All too soon the children's adventure was over, the sun was sinking lower in the sky turning the cliff face a pale golden colour, it was time for the journey home.

Chapter 37

On Sunday 3rd September 1939 the radio broadcast by Neville Chamberlain declared, "This morning the British ambassador in Berlin handed the German government a final note stating that, unless we hear from them by 11 o'clock that they were prepared at once to withdraw their troops from Poland, a state of war would exist between us. I have to tell you now that no such undertaking has been received and that consequently this country is at war with Germany".

In order to try to make the British weak, the Germans tried to cut off supplies of food as well as other goods. The ships that were trying to bring food to Britain were attacked many times by German submarines. Because of this, rationing was introduced to make sure that everyone had a fair share of the items that were hard to get hold of during the war. On National Registration Day on 29th September 1939, every householder had to fill in a form giving details of the people who lived in their house. Using the information gathered, the government issued every one with an identity card and ration book. The books contained coupons that had to be signed by or handed to the shopkeeper every time rationed goods were bought. Later on clothes rationing began because there was a shortage of materials to make clothes. The coupon system allowed people to buy one complete, new set of clothes once a year.

Rationing made very little difference to Lillian and Percy. Living in the country and working on the farm, eggs and milk were always available and Lillian made her own butter from the cream of the milk. Percy grew his own vegetables and they ate a lot of bread, it was filling and large loaf cost only a few pennies.

When time allowed, Lillian would walk into Folkestone to a shop that would take children's clothes that they had outgrown and swap them for larger ones. Nothing was thrown away if it could be exchanged or altered, even old jumpers were unwound and the wool used again. When garments were past mending Lillian was always on the lookout for the rag and bone man and would hand over her sack of clothes. With the exchange done, Lillian would buy some sprats or sometimes a pair of kippers. At other times when the bundle of rags she had been saving consisted of only two or three items, the rag and bone man wouldn't give her any money but instead would give her a two day old chick. This would be placed it in a box filled with newspaper to keep it warm and when it was old enough, the growing chick would be put out into the garden and fattened up for a meal.

The British wartime drive for self-sufficiency was *"make do and mend"* which was what they did and through Percy's hard work and Lillian's frugalness, their children always had clothes on their backs and although they were sometimes hungry as were the rest of the country, they never starved.

October 1940 came to a close and with it the offer of a larger house - Jacques Court a mile down the lane from Stone Cottage.

The parlour, which Lillian said was to be her best room and only used on special occasions had a small open grate fire with a dresser on one side. "Just the thing" she thought "for putting my china on." Above the fire place, a well chipped mantelpiece which would be home for a couple of cheap china dogs that Hilda had given her. On the far wall of the scullery was another fire with bars at the front and little oven at the side. Next to this was something Lillian had often wished for, an old mangle. It needed some attention but that wasn't a problem, Percy got to work and soon water was squeezed out between two heavy wooden rollers that were turned with a handle. With six people all wanting clean clothes wash days would now be a little easier for Lillian. The rooms at Jacques Court were slightly larger plus there was an extra bedroom which the family desperately needed. All the rooms had been whitewashed over the bare brick walls and apart from the area over and around the fireplaces which were black with smoke, the rooms were quite clean. A galvanized bucket toilet with a nail pushed into the wall from where the squares of newspaper hung, was situated at the end of the garden. When the toilet was near to overflowing Percy would dig a hole in the garden and empty the contents of the bucket into it.

By mid November the house was freezing. The larger rooms took longer to heat and Percy knew that if he used too much fuel on a daily basis, it would not last the winter. Buying more wasn't an option the household budget just wouldn't stretch that far. In the hope that it would make the scullery a little warmer Lillian made a rag rug to cover part of the cold bare brick floor. Hunting through their old clothes she made two piles, one for use in making her rug, the other for the rag and bone man. A sack cut in half lengthways was used as the underside of the rug. Every evening the children would sit tearing strips of old rags and laying them neatly in a pile on the floor ready for Lillian to use the following day.

It took her two weeks and hundreds of stitches to finish the rug, by which time her fingers were so sore she would wince in pain. The rug was nowhere near big enough to cover even half the tiny floor area and done little to stop the chill of the house but it was bright and added a much needed cheerfulness against the blackout curtains of the room.

How they all looked forward to Sunday afternoon, the only time the "best room" was unlocked and a fire lit in the grate. It was here that they ate their Sunday tea. This was the day the children had bread and margarine as well as jam or paste followed by a small cake. Afterwards they sat round the fire with warm hands and feet while Lillian read them a passage from the Bible.

The old saying "new house, new baby" came true when Lillian and Percy's last child, a son who they named John, was born.

This was also the year that Hilda decided to take her fight for Florence to a much higher level.

Chapter 38

Twenty Seven Years Earlier:

Florence was just 11 years old, still a child but old enough to know what she wanted and she really did want to live with Mrs Bridges. The young girl's home, Potts Farm at Ash, Kent was a far cry from the huge depressing walls of the Workhouse. Her appointed visitor from the Union, Nina Jackson visited once a month and her report read:

Date of visit and last previous visit.	Feb 14th /Jan 14th
Child's condition?	Good
Training and influences in home satisfactory.	Yes
Home satisfactory?	Yes
Sleeping accommodation?	Good
Any Complaints?	No, only that the boots sent did not fit.

When Florence first arrived at Mrs Bridges home, she was disobedient and disrespectful but Mrs Bridges soon came to learn why. The young girl had no recollection of ever having been kissed by her mother and this was etched into her face, a face that spoke of misery, confusion and suppression. A face of child who had never been loved and had only seen the frightening side of life.

During the months that followed Florence changed completely and Mrs Bridges took great delight in watching the tiny dark girl become less rude and more helpful. She was also grateful that Florence was helping her to paper over the cracks in her miserable loveless marriage and for several months, Mrs Bridges lavished all the love her husband refused on the vulnerable child.

All too soon the happiness Florence had experienced was gone again.

Even though the house was still beautiful and she still had her own bedroom with a soft bed, fancy drapes and a cupboard full of lovely clothes, none of this made any difference to the young, lonely girl. Mrs Bridges had left.

Once again Florence's thoughts tuned to her sisters. She wanted to feel their hands take hers or their arms wrapped round her shoulders, then she would know that she was loved.

Florence soon went back to her old habits and was rude and disobedient doing everything she could to annoy the new woman of the house. It was obvious that the woman disliked her and Florence positively hated the woman. In her mind, it was she that had sent Mrs Bridges away.

By September the woman of the house had had enough, could not cope with a child that would not obey her and wouldn't even appear humble while being chastised. Florence would hold her head up and stare her straight in the eye with a look that would never waver. Even when being physically punished the stare was just the same, no tears in fact not even a tremble of a lip, just a stare. The woman found this all quite unnerving. She knew about, but had no understanding of what Florence had been through in her short life.

On February 15th of the following year the report given to the Workhouse read:

Florence Hatcher
Boarded with Mrs Bridges but is now back in the Union.
Date of last and previous visit.   July 3rd/Feb 14th
Child's condition satisfactory.   No
House and training influences.   Unsatisfactory

Mrs Bridges had moved since my last visit and as I did not consider the house satisfactory Florence was removed and is now in the Wash house pending her reception by the Waifs and Strays
Nina Jackson. (Appointed visitor)

Two weeks after being returned to the workhouse, application forms were filled out and signed by the church minister and other concerned members of the community and Florence was taken to her new abode, a Home for Waifs and Strays in Surrey.

The Waifs and Strays' Society was founded in 1881 by Edward Rudolf a civil servant, and his brother Robert, a Sunday school teacher in South Lambeth, London. The home in Cheam was built in 1913, one of the quickest to be completed. It opened in 1914 and took girls aged six to sixteen. By the main entrance, being looked after by a stern faced nurse was a group of young children playing on the lawns.

As Florence was led up the steps to the large wooden entrance door she turned and looked at the nurse and in return received a smile that changed the stern look completely, causing tiny crinkles to appear round the nurse's eyes and mouth. Florence liked being at Cheam but the longing to see her sisters never diminished. Often she would sit on the window seat so that she could see them straight away, should they come to visit. After a year Florence gave up looking, unaware that her sisters were still looking for her.

The teachers at Cheam believed and stressed on the girls that by giving them an education they would lead a better life in the future. Florence worked hard and became one of the best pupils in her class. After school the children and staff would walk to the chapel at the side of the home to pray, for Florence though the highlight of the week was Sunday school where she soaked up every word from the Bible.

Three meals a day, eaten in silence in the communal dining room were nicely cooked and always served piping hot. Next to the dining room was a large kitchen where the children, as part of their chores would help with the cleaning and tidying. Their reward was to have any leftover pudding.

The dormitories were large and airy and the bed clothes always clean. It was the responsibility of the girls to keep the room neat and tidy with no items of clothing on the bed or the floor. It was here after lights out that Florence and her friends would whisper and giggle until one by one they fell asleep. Her passed life was a distant memory now, erased by the feeling of being cared for and being spoken to as a human being. Nobody mentioned her colour or called her names. She went to the seaside and sat on the sand with the other girls watching Punch and Judy. Every year she took part in the traditional dancing round the maypole.

Florence was encouraged by the matron to join the Brownies and later the Guides and the young girl succeeded in winning badges for activities such as laundry and cooking, and domestic work.

Often Florence was taken on outings by the people from the local community. Most times it was only for a walk in the park to feed the ducks and watch the dragonflies skimming across the pond but how she looked forward to those days. At last she was happy.

The house in Cheam with its very strict but fair regime was home to Florence for the next four years. During this time she blossomed into a considerate polite and obedient teenager. She loved being there and had a fondness for all the staff; they always had time to listen to a trouble or a worry. Florence tried not to think about the day when, at sixteen, she would have to leave, thinking about that made her head ache and her tummy flip. Inevitably though, that day arrived. The previous week there had been talks given by the Matron to all the children that were leaving the home on how to conduct themselves whilst working.

"You girls will be employed indoors as under-cooks, ladies' maids, parlour maids or general servants. When summoned to a particular room by your employer, you will knock gently and wait until told to enter. When leaving the room do so quietly, with your head bowed slightly.

Never speak unless spoken to and then address your employers as Sir or Ma'am. If you should overhear any conversation between the master and his family, do not repeat it. When you receive your wage save most of it, spend a little and never borrow or lend and you will learn how to manage your money.

Should you find employment in the larger houses or estates, you will find many men employed as grooms, gardeners, carpenters, blacksmiths and also as chauffeurs. You will socialise with some of these people and we at this home have instilled in you the importance of behaving in a correct and proper manner.

Remember our teachings. No not sniff, always use a handkerchief .Do not blow your nose in public, wipe it gently. While sitting, place your hands in your lap, back upright and straight with your legs neatly crossed at the ankle. When standing, your head should be high, your shoulders back and your stomach in. Pronounce every word clearly and correctly when in conversation. Speak softly and never blaspheme."

All these things a mother should have taught them. Most of the girls living there had no mothers and those that did, including Florence had no idea where they were.

Chapter 39

As her first step away from a life in homes and institutions, Florence was sent to a hostel in Maidstone, Kent. She missed the girls that she had known at Cheam, but was happily employed in one of the fashionable coffee houses and had become friendly with many people. She loved working there.

Going back to the hostel after her shifts had finished was what she hated. There, girls commented on her thick black tight curls and her dark skin. Some stared at her. Others whispered about her. Others made monkey noises and movements whenever they saw her. Her stomach felt tight and knotted, she felt she couldn't breathe.

The awful headaches that she hadn't had for years now returned with a vengeance. Florence couldn't cope with the name calling and wished they would leave her alone. She would lash out at her tormentors, which made them laugh and call her names even more. Slowly she could feel her temper rising and as the taunts became longer and more frequent, so the pounding in her head became worse. Every morning when she awoke she would vow to herself that whatever happened and no matter what was said to her, she would not get angry.

After only five weeks, her temper having got the better of her again Florence was back in Eastry Workhouse. In order to assess her mind and mental stability doctors came and asked her questions but they could get her to say nothing, despite punishments ranging from loss of food, loss of free time and being given extra chores. Nothing made any difference; Florence would not speak to anyone. Inside her head though, she silently screamed for her siblings and a mother she could not even remember.

Both the professional and medical authorities decided there was nothing wrong with the girl, that she was just being awkward. Consequently a job as a laundry maid at the House of Sacred Passion in Hastings was found for Florence. She would be provided with board and lodging plus 1s 3d per week. On the 6th June 1924 with the screaming still echoing in her head and her stomach so knotted it made her feel sick, she was escorted to her place of work and introduced to the matron and other staff.

The first few weeks went quite well for Florence at Hastings, she spoke in a respectful manner to her superiors, was spotlessly clean in her habits and went about her work in a quiet methodical manner. She loved being busy, muddled thoughts of her family were kept at bay when she was working. Lying in her bed at night though, thoughts of them filled her head.

"Have they returned to Eastry yet?", "Do they remember me?", "What do they look like?", "Will they recognize me, will I recognize them?", "I wonder what mother looks like. Is she looking for me?"

Endless sleepless nights spent wondering and worrying.

A slim, swarthy skinned, dark haired girl was admitted to the Priory Road Home in October 1924. She was 13 years old, the same age as Lillian when Florence had last seen her. She gazed at the girl and the voice in Florence's mind shouted out to her "It's your sister, she's found you." She ran to the girl embracing her and kissing her cheeks while the girl tried to push her away. Laughing and then more screaming took turns to invade Florence's head. She could feel her heart banging against her ribs as if it was trying to escape. The room spun out of control followed by merciful darkness as she passed out.

When Florence regained consciousness she was in bed with the matron and a nurse standing over her.

She drank the strong sweet tea and asked in-between sips, "Where is my sister Lillian now, is she allowed to come in and see me?"

"Now Florence, you know that your sister isn't here don't you?" explained the matron.

"Don't say that, please don't say that. She is here, she has come to take me home!" screamed Florence, "I saw her. You are nothing but a liar."

Chapter 40

Florence Hatcher was returned to Eastry Workhouse on 28th October 1924, the reason given: Infirmity.

She felt she had returned home, the only "home" she could really remember.

"All she had to do now," she thought, "was to wait for her sisters to come home." They would come for her soon, she just knew they would.

Each week the local doctor would come and question Florence about her thoughts. "Did she know what day of the week it was?"

"Did she have nightmares?"

"Did she ever feel angry?"

The answers she gave were all positive. The screaming and pounding in her head stopped when she was at Eastry Workhouse. After four months, the doctor could find nothing wrong with her apart from a flash of anger from her chocolate brown eyes whenever the subject of her colour was mentioned. He was beginning to find the weekly sessions with this not unintelligent girl quite boring. He suggested to the workhouse master that Florence should make some type of contribution to life and find some useful employment.

The Reverend Wilson Carlile founded the Church Army in 1882 and it had been at the heart of Evangelism within the established church ever since. The aim of the Church Army was to take the news of Jesus to those "unfortunate people, the most lost" that would not normally had known about the Church and its teachings.

In 1925 Florence was sent to The Church Army House at Old Southgate in London on the orders of the workhouse master. She was to work hard, receive discipline, while at the same time having religious guidance in the hope that it would "calm her and lessen the anger she feels within"

A popular young woman, everything was going well for Florence until two weeks later when the taunts began again. "Sambo, Coon, Monkey face".

The old demons came back to Florence with a vengeance, pounding headaches with screaming voices somewhere in her head.

Two days later, Florence was found laughing hysterically whilst throwing everything she could lay her hands on crashing to the floor. Kicking out at anyone who came near her and screaming at her tormentors to leave her alone. Suddenly the hysterical laughter stopped and the tears that followed were tears that should have fallen when, as a young child she had watched her mother walk away and leave her at the Workhouse.

Florence changed during the following few days.

The next time she heard the word "coon", she slapped her tormentor so hard the girl was knocked to the ground. Now she had that girl sorted out, Florence began encouraging any of the other girls that would listen to be rebellious.

She would lie in bed in the mornings until a member of staff physically removed her. Once they had managed to remove her from the bed, Florence would sit in the chair like a rag doll while they tried to dress her. She tried to escape via the dormitory window one night at the same time encouraging the other girls to do the same. She was caught before reaching the gate at the end of the drive. Her behaviour became so bad that on the 16th of September 1925, the Matron wrote to Eastry Workhouse stating:

"Sirs,
We are unable to do anything with regard the training of Florence Elsie Hatcher. She prefers the workhouse to the home and I am asking the Board to fetch her from this home as soon as possible. Her influence over the other girls is now getting out of hand. It is unfair, not only on me but also my staff to be expected to deal with such a person."

She then called Florence into her office and told her that a letter had been sent to the Board at Eastry Workhouse and just as soon as was possible Florence would be returned there. This was just the news that the troubled 18 year old wanted to hear. Her sisters would know where to find her now. She knew they would be looking for her. Once she knew she was going back to Eastry, Florence's response to anyone in authority that tried asking, telling or ordering her what to do was, "Bugger off!" or "Sod you."

On the 18th September, a telegram was sent via the matron of the Queen Elizabeth Lodge to Eastry Workhouse this time stating:

"Sirs,
I must warn you, Hatcher must leave at once. She is intolerable.
I will expect an Officer to fetch her tomorrow. If no one comes, she shall be removed from here and she will travel alone."

After spending just 20 days at the Lodge, Florence was to be returned to Eastry Workhouse.

Daylight slowly crept though the window of Florence's room, she had been awake since 4.30am, waiting for the officer from Eastry. He arrived at 12.30 and after talks with the matron and clutching some paperwork outlining Florence's behaviour he clicked his fingers at her indicating they were leaving. The September day was quite pleasant with a warm breeze and local residents could be seen enjoying a pleasant walk along the lanes. Florence though was oblivious to most of what was around her, she just wanted to get back to Eastry.

She was however, very aware of the coolness between her and the Officer.

She resented his authority.

He resented having to fetch her.

Chapter 41

Dr Collis of the Chartham Mental Hospital assisted by two colleagues examined Florence on October the 24th 1925 after a request by the master of Eastry Workhouse. The doctor authorized Florence's detention to a mental hospital.

"It is," he said, "the best place for you at the moment, there will be other feeble minded people there as well as other coloured people. For my paperwork, could you tell me was it you mother or father or maybe both that were of colour"?

Florence said in reply,

"Find out yourself about the colour of my parents. You must surely realise that I can remember nothing of them. If you are so intelligent why you are asking me questions, why don't you just read my file, I'm sure those details are in it."

She sat it the chair opposite these "experts" and stared at all three of them with utter contempt.

Dr Collis ignored Florence's outburst, but scribbled furiously on his note pad before informing her that he was going to conduct an "intelligence test."

She felt like screaming at the doctor that she wasn't feeble minded and she just wasn't going to answer any more of their stupid questions.

The mental hospital near Canterbury had opened in 1875, costing in the region of £240,000 the all-brick building consisted of a central entrance, with offices and a committee room. A chapel stood in the centre with two blocks on either side, with another six at the back and held approximately 1000 men and women.

Florence hated the place as soon as she laid eyes on it, an ugly grey sprawl overlooking the church in a little village. Her first two days were spent wandering the endless corridors wishing she could find a way out. On the third day at 9.30am she was summoned to the medical room and told to sit in front of a desk, behind which sat three different Doctors, all asking her the same old questions. After every question was answered, she pleaded with them,

"Please let me return to Eastry, I didn't choose to be separated from my sisters and I miss them so much. I know my mind will be calm and well once I find them. Really, I am not mad or crazy, please help me."

No help came. Instead "mentally defective/feeble minded" was the degrading and humiliating label bestowed on Florence.

After the questioning, came the medication, after-which Florence was taken to the day room. The room had grey chairs placed methodically around the outside, not one of them out of line, like an army of metal soldiers. The occupied chairs held souls that had once been proud, upright people, the heads of their houses, the breadwinners, the homemakers. There were husbands, fathers, brothers and sons. Wives, mothers, sisters and daughters all sat staring into space with eyes that were dulled, vacant and unseeing. Some sat too frightened to move, upright and rigid as if made from stone. Others were wringing their hands together in a continuous circular movement. Several others were rocking their upper body to and fro, some gently, others with an element of aggression.

Florence was vaguely aware of being sat quite roughly onto one of the hard cold chairs. Her mouth felt dry and waves of nausea swept over her. She dearly wanted a cup of water but, although she opened her mouth, no words came out. She tried desperately to hold her head up but it hurt so much. Just before the state of semi-consciousness took hold of her, she felt her head roll forward and to her horror realised she was dribbling and could do nothing about it. After her head had cleared, she was still in the hard grey chair, opposite the grey walls and all around her were people with grey faces, people who really did need medication. She made a vow to herself right then that if she were to be given any more treatment, she would make sure she made it as difficult as possible for the medical staff to administer it to her.

And she did. At every weekly treatment session, Florence kicked and swore and lashed out at anyone who approached her. Isolation cells and shackles which were called 'quiet rooms' and 'restraints' were used in order to make Florence comply. Sometimes these methods worked but more often than not they didn't and Florence, strapped into a chair and with thick swirling fog crowding the inside of her head, would watch them all, studying and analysing her.

A young woman now, Florence could not understand what was happening to her, she had been institutionalised for so long with little outside stimulation and no family love. Her life had become a circle of confusion and bleakness. How could these people prescribe and administer drugs for her against her will? Why couldn't they understand that she just felt a great sadness over being parted from her family and just wanted to find them?

Florence told anyone that would listen, that she didn't have mental problems; all she needed was someone to understand her feelings. Unfortunately for Florence, many of the staff had little or no training in how to communicate with the patients about their problems. The doctor hardly listened to what Florence had told him when she was admitted to the hospital, he just made a few observations, jotted down some notes and prescribed the treatment.

Two years later having not responded to the legally allowed treatment, nothing further could be done for her and Florence was informed that she was being sent to yet another institution. Fighting the urge to cry she finally broke down, detesting the fact that she was unwanted, weak and scared.

Chapter 42

Under the Mental Deficiency Act hospitals became "colonies" designed to separate defectives from the country's gene pool. A section of this act stated that "mental defectiveness" meant a condition of incomplete development of the mind existing before the age of eighteen and the following classes of people who are mentally defective will fall under one of the following categories.

Idiots: those with such a degree of mental defectiveness, that they are unable to guard themselves against physical dangers.

Imbeciles: persons in who exists mental defectiveness which though not amounting to idiocy they are incapable of managing themselves or their affairs.

The feeble minded: people in whose case there exists mental defectiveness, though not imbeciles still they require care, supervision and control for their own protection or for the protection of others.

Moral defectives: persons where there is mental defectiveness with strongly vicious or criminal tendencies and who require supervision and control for the protection of others.

Theories regarding mental health and the colour of the skin had been put forward over many years. Dr. Samuel Cartwright, a white American physician, created a mental illness peculiar to Black people.

He stated: *"Negroes trying to gain freedom by running away from their owners is a symptom of a serious mental disease called Drapetomania"*. He suggested that this condition could be cured by recapturing the 'patient', rubbing him down with oil and beating him into submission.

In 1869 the English psychologist Francis Galton published *Hereditary Genius* and he too made it clear that he took a racist view of Blacks when he wrote:

"On average the intellectual standard of a Negro is some two grades below our own."

Darenth Asylum and Schools became Darenth Industrial Training Colony in about 1911 where *"mental defectives of a higher-grade"* were taught crafts and industrial skills as well as moral and intellectual education to improve the mind, physical education to improve the low organisation, and industrial education in order to contribute towards their maintenance.

The building consisted of a main administrative block, with a laundry and the kitchens to the back. The boys accommodation was to the east and the girls on the west side. The remainder of the block was made up of school rooms, dormitories, a recreation room, a chapel and a receiving office. This was Florence's next "home".

She tried hard to fit in with the other people there, and tried even harder to enhance the hazy visions of her sisters in her mind. It had been such a long time since she had last seen them and this, coupled with the electric treatment, dimmed her mind so much she could barley remember what they looked like at all. Was Lillian taller than Irene? Who was the eldest? Who had the grey eyes, was that Irene? Was it Lillian? Who held their head up high and stared, directly at whoever was telling them off, Lillian or Irene or both of them?

Two and a half years of racial insults, harsh treatment and the deep feeling of being alone in the world, coupled with a longing for her family and the overwhelming need to be loved came to a head one morning in 1929. Florence was 22 years old.

The first week of November 1929 was the wettest of the century for England and Wales, rain fell constantly nearly every day, forming miniature streams that rushed down the roadside forming tiny bubbles, topped with a dirty froth. Heavy raindrops ran down the tall windows of the bleak building that was home to the troubled souls that most of the country had forgotten.

Florence stood at the window tracing the raindrops as they hit the window before weaving their way to the bottom of the pane. In the distance she could just make out the blurred outlines of people going about their daily business, heads down, shoulders hunched against the relentless downpour. One old man pushing his barrow, was nearly bent double trying to manoeuvre the wheels through the shallower depths of the water. Several times he stopped and wrung water from the sodden dirty sacks covering his barrow under which lay his precious wares that he so desperately needed to sell in order to buy his next meal.

She had no idea how long she had been standing there when a hand snaked out from nowhere landing with full force on the side of Florence's cheek and the voice of her main tormentor's words began to fill her head. This person had goaded Florence at every opportunity, had pinched her so hard that her skin had been broken and tiny drops of blood had formed. On seeing the blood, her tormentor scathingly told her,

"I am really surprised to see such red blood coming from such a dark person, didn't think you darkies had blood in your veins."

This same person ensured that Florence was made to do the worst of the jobs around the colony, smirking as she said,

"You coons are only fit for cleaning toilets. No one would be able to see if any of the contents of the toilets are on you it would just blend in with your skin colour Florence. As for the smell, you darkies stink anyway."

Her hair was pulled at with such force it came out by the handful, much to her assailant's glee. On and on went the insults and bullying. Everything around Florence seemed dark and cold—so utterly bleak—as if her life was slipping into a dark cave.

On one occasion Florence tried to tell the matron of the awful things that were happening. Having called the member of staff into her office the Matron said sternly, "I have had a complaint regarding your conduct regarding the Hatcher woman."

"Matron, I treat all of the people here with the same respect, has anyone else complained about me, or is it just Hatcher?" enquired the staff member innocently.

"Are you telling me that you have not used inappropriate words in reference to her skin colour or that you make her do all the worst jobs?"

"Matron, I vehemently deny any wrong doing at all, Hatcher is nothing but a troublesome liar," came the reply.

Florence was told not to make such wicked accusations again.

Life for this woman was a living hell. Nothing seemed to matter anymore but still the screams of despair in her head told Florence to stand up for herself, put a stop to all this.

Two days later, breakfast having been eaten, Florence was scrubbing the tables when she realised her tormentor had walked back into the dining room.

"Well, Sambo," she said, "your little chat with matron didn't do you any good all, did it?"

Florence said nothing.

"Answer me, you black bitch," hissed her tormentor.

Clenching her fists to her sides, Florence left the table she was cleaning,

"Just where do you think you are going?" her tormentor shouted. "You should ask permission to leave a superior's presence, and I am your superior, you monkey faced nigger. Get back here now."

Florence carried on walking, but halfway across the dining room her tormentor caught up with her. Holding a clump of Florence's hair in one hand, she pulled down making sure Florence's head was leaning backwards. Making a fist with her other hand she punched Florence just under her chin, knocking out two teeth and splitting her lips and tongue.

With tears filling her eyes, Florence went into the kitchen picked up the nearest utensil she could find and turn to face the woman that had robbed her of her last ounce of self esteem. A second later the smirk on the woman's face had turned to complete fear.

Chapter 43

Rampton Hospital in Nottinghamshire had opened in 1910 as England's second State Institution for mentally defective people who were considered to be responsible for very serious crimes. The high security at Rampton was designed to detain patients who, if at large, would pose a risk to others in the community. The institution comprised of three central wards and was home to over 120 men and women and staffed by approximately 20 attendants and nurses. In time Rampton Hospital became known as "The Broadmoor of the North".

The Criminal Act made provisions for the safe custody of persons who were of unsound mind and who were:

a) Charged with treason, murder or felony, who were acquitted because of insanity

b) Indicted and found insane at the time of arraignment

c) Brought before any criminal court to be discharged for want of prosecution who appeared insane.

d) Apprehended under circumstances denoting a derangement of mind and a purpose to commit an indictable offence.

His Majesty could issue an order stating the manner and place in which the person was confined. This meant that the Home Office determined what happened to the person. Such persons detained under any order or authority of the Home Office could not be freed by the commissioners.

Florence was admitted to Rampton on the 11th November 1929 after hearing:

"The sentence of the court is custody for a period of years which the court specifies as a period of 50 years. That means that your case will not be considered by the Parole Board until you have served at least that amount of years in custody. After which the Parole Board will be entitled to consider your release. When satisfied that you no longer need be confined in custody for the protection of the public it will be able to direct your release. Until then you will remain in custody.

If you are released, it will be that you are subject to a licence for the rest of your life and liable to be recalled at any time if your licence is revoked, either on the recommendation of the Parole Board, or, if it is thought to be in the public interest, by the Secretary of State."

Florence's first glimpse of Rampton was from the back of a large van. A huge building suddenly loomed into sight, enormous stone steps leading to a huge main door. Once inside the main door, Florence was left shackled to a table in the reception office while her accompanying officer went in search of the sister – in –charge.

After being led through endless corridors with low ceilings and bars at every window they reached the medical office where Florence was asked more questions, checked for hair and body lice, stripped, measured and weighed.

Afterwards she was given a shapeless coarse dress and put into a cell which contained an old chamber pot, a locker and an iron bed. The metal door, with its thick glass observation window at the top and a dense mesh screen below to enable communication, slammed shut as she was pushed inside.

The bathroom, at the end of the corridor held two baths between which a nurse would stand looking the patients up and down, passing remarks about their bodies. Privacy for the patients was not on the agenda. Punishments were.

Favourite punishments included being throttled with keychains and the cold-water-towel treatment. This involved the towel being soaked in freezing water, twisted and used to hit the patients when they misbehaved.

Sometimes the more troublesome patients were taken from their ward and put in an isolation room where there was nothing but a rubber chamber pot and just two rugs that served as a bed.

Within the first few days of being in Rampton, Florence had witnessed these forms of punishment. Escape, she knew, was impossible, everywhere she went she was observed. Every door she stepped through was firmly closed behind her.

Although she was now 22 years old, Florence needed her sisters more than ever, she felt so alone. Alone and frightened. Rampton was worse than anything she had ever imagined, it was a place that nightmares were made of. Florence was soon experiencing different types of "cures" which consisted of drugs, drugs and even more drugs. They made her feel as though her head was trapped in a spinning top. Sanity would be her salvation one moment, then suddenly it was gone and she would be pulled back down to the murky shadows.

When the drugs failed to make much of a difference, Florence was given electric shock treatment as well.

She was taken to a room with about six other patients, where they were all strapped to treatment tables. The other patients watched in terror as the doctor placed conducting paste on Florence's temples while the young woman passively accepted the rubber mouthpiece, which was to prevent cuts during the seizure, pushed into her mouth.

On a small box was a button which the doctor had been adjusting. When she was quite satisfied that the level of power was correct she pressed the button and the convulsion began.

Florence's body went rigid and then began to convulse. Her convulsing muscles prevented her from breathing and her face turned a ghastly blue. Although it was only a matter of seconds, it seemed ages before she could catch her breath again. She knew there was nothing she could do about the saliva mixed with blood and green bile that frothed in the corners of her mouth or the fact that she was making snorting and grunting sounds.

Once the treatment had finished for the day Florence felt so confused and dazed that she forgot many things and for a few weeks her emotional problems were diminished, but they were not solved in any way. They were forever just under the surface of her mind.

(Today if one received an accidental shock, perhaps by touching their head against a short-circuited electrical appliance and suffered a convulsion they would be rushed to the nearest hospital and treated as an emergency. If they woke confused, dazed, disoriented and complaining of a headache and nausea they would be kept in hospital for careful observation.)

After her first session of this treatment Florence was sure she was going to die and voiced this fear to the staff. She was told, "Shut up, you're doing fine, don't make such a fuss".

It wasn't long before Florence started to show the classic adverse reaction to the cocktail of drugs that she had been forced to take, rocking herself backwards and forwards, constantly darting her tongue in and out of her mouth, her body twitching and shaking.

After 15 ECT shocks on alternate days Florence's mind and body accepted all that she could not change and she went to her treatments meekly and without complaint. Only after the doctors deemed that she was "controllable" did her treatment cease.

Chapter 44

Outdoor recreation times were spent walking the "airing courts" for thirty minutes, walking 'round and 'round once in circles, once or twice a day, depending on the weather watched over by a member of staff. So as to cheer and calm the patients, the "airing courts" or enclosed yards were laid out to enhance or create a pleasant view with a few shrubs, trees and flower borders.

Florence soon began to look forward to these walks, she loved hearing the sounds of the birds singing to each other while the leaves on the trees whispered to her as light breezes floated through them.

Gradually over a period of time, conditions and treatments at Rampton changed for the better as staff, some of whom were cruel and unfeeling, were replaced by those who were better trained. These properly trained staff accepted Florence for who she was; no one mentioned her colour, called her names or pulled her hair. No one shunned her and she wasn't made to do anything that the paler skinned patients were not required to do. She learned to smile again, and would hum little tunes to herself as she went about her daily routines. Occasionally thoughts of her sisters would come to her and the old sadness would try to creep in. Now though, instead of giving vent to the raging anger that in the past had altered her life completely, she would carry on smiling and humming whilst thinking "one day I will see my sisters".

Florence had no memory of her elder half sister Hilda, but it was she who six weeks later made the first of many applications for her discharge. The application was unsuccessful.

The years went by and Florence knew the medical staff were doing all they could to try and help her and it was help she now accepted. Recreational studies were held every day and Florence enjoyed going to sewing classes and loved the dance classes she attended. In the outside world young people flocked to dance halls and jazz clubs most evenings. Inside Rampton, Florence danced one evening a week, while the patients who had "two left feet" sat and watched. Not for her the fashionable clothes of the era but she still loved showing the other patients how she could do the Shimmy, the Charleston and the Black Bottom.

She learned to play the piano and would often give recitals to the other patients some of whom would hum along with Florence's music. Each November the patients would spend much of their recreational time making crepe paper decorations. The floor would be covered with pots of paste and paper of every colour. Some patients would tear the paper into petal shapes and using the glue would create bunches of flowers. Others would tear strips of the different coloured paper and weave them together to form bows and streamers. As Christmas Eve approached their creations would be hung in one of the halls, transforming it from a cold bare institution into something quite spectacular. Florence loved Christmas Day and after prayers and carol singing in the main hall the discipline of normal routine became more relaxed for a while.

Patients gave their handmade Christmas cards to the nurses, doctors and to each other. Those that were able joined in the festivities, some playing games, others dancing while others just sat, looking and feeling bewildered.

Everyone was given small gifts of hankies and socks or stockings, an orange, an apple and some chocolate squares or sweets, The same gifts each year but they bought with them expectation and excitement. Christmas dinner was a grand affair, with goose and plum pudding followed by two cups of tea.

Each year they all agreed it was a far better Christmas than any of the previous ones.

Florence made friends with many of the people in hospital and as the news of sterilisation of the feeble-minded slowly seeped through the corridors of Rampton she had nothing but sympathy with the unmarried mothers who were convinced that they would be among the first to have the controversial operation. Sterilisation of the feeble-minded had first been spoken about in about 1910, and now the campaign was the talk of the hospital, it was said by several of the nurses that Britain was on the brink of introducing the law.

Winston Churchill was a supporter of this law and part of his letter written to the Prime Minister reportedly stated.

"The unnatural and increasingly rapid growth of the feebleminded classes, together with a steady restriction among all the thrifty and superior stocks, constitutes a race danger. I feel that the source from which the stream of madness is fed should be cut off and sealed up before another year has passed."

At the last moment, to the relief of thousands the recommendations were dropped.

Chapter 45

While Florence was trying to live her life within the walls of Rampton Hospital her sisters were still fighting for her release. For years they fought, writing to the Home Secretaries of the time:

*"22, Granville Street,
Dover,
Kent*

Sir,
I am writing to beg your help in releasing my sister Florence Elsie Hatcher, from the confines of Rampton Hospital.
It is true she is guilty of having a bad temper and striking out at someone, but this incident was caused by her being physically and verbally provoked. She has never been dangerous or insane.
Her character has been determined by the environment she has been subjected to since she was just five years old. She should have been taken care of by our mother and treated with understanding and love. She wasn't, none of us were. Why? We will never know.

Florence has four siblings who, in their own way, have all coped with the hardships that life has handed them. Florence found it more difficult, which led her on the downward path to Rampton.

Does she really deserve to be incarcerated for the rest of her life? Hasn't she suffered enough?
We, her siblings, are sure that if Florence had been better represented at her first court appearance, the outcome would have been different.

I will gladly offer her a home with me and my family, if this appeal succeeds. I will take responsibility for her in conjunction with her probation officer and ensure that any medical issues were promptly dealt with.

As human beings we all have the gift of many things including compassion sympathy and pity. We are sure that you Sir have these gifts, as well as the power to prevent our sister from further suffering.

I remain,
Yours sincerely,

Hilda Grace Gillett."

Two successive Home Secretaries, Samuel John Gurney Hoare, Home Secretary 1937–9 and John Anderson Home Secretary 1939-1940 dismissed their appeal and with each dismissal Hilda and Lillian became more determined that they would never give up their fight for their sister's release.

In September 1942 Herbert Morrison the Home Secretary of the time listened. The son of a police officer he had lost the sight of his right eye at a very young age, had little formal education, left school at 14 and became an errand boy. Morrison was in office from October 1940 until May 1945.

Parole Boards were attended by Florence and transcripts from the original case hearing were applied for, every word in every sentence methodically read. Weeks turned into months, months into years.

On 5th October 1944, Florence was released on license into her sister's care after nearly 31 years in institutions. There was no need for celebration. She had the warmth and love of her family. That was all she had ever wanted.

She was home at last.

Florence

These are our ancestors, some of whom we never knew but all of them in some small way have enriched our lives and taught us many lessons. We wrote this book in the hope that their stories are never allowed to slip beneath the sands of time and be forgotten.

From them we learned that although some circumstances and background may have influenced who we are, the future is in our own hands.

The year is now 2008. Florence and our other ancestors have been physically absent from our family for many years, but their descendents, all from different walks of life, are scattered around the world. To those descendents who may have wondered about their origins, these are your roots.

CERTIFICATE OF ANCESTRY

African Ancestry hereby certifies that

Jill Williams

Shares Maternal Genetic Ancestry with

the Tuareg people in Niger

Based on a MatriClan™
analysis performed on
April 24, 2003

Nick Kittles, Ph.D.
Scientific Director